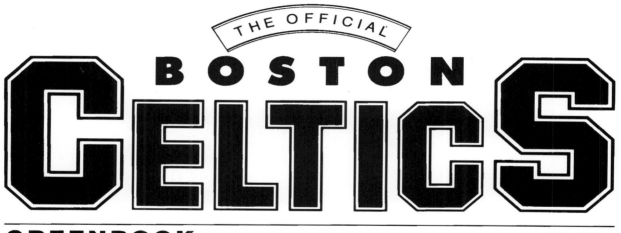

THE OFFICIAL BOSTON CELTICS

GREENBOOK '91-'92

by Roland Lazenby

photographs by Steve Lipofsky

Celtics Profiles and Records by David Zuccaro

Jefferson Street Press

The leaky Garden roof forced a postponement of the December game with Atlanta.

Design by Karen Snidow Lazenby

©1991, Roland Lazenby

ISBN 0-87833-032-1

Printed in the United States of America

Contents

Gavitt and Auerbach talk hoops.

Preface

Welcome to the fourth editon of the *Boston Celtics Greenbook*. As he has for the past three editions, Steve Lipofsky, through his excellent photography, offers a classic view of the NBA's winningest team. His work captures every element of Boston Garden's wonderful atmosphere, all the seriousness and humor and drama.

For history, we turn to long-time NBA photographer Ron Koch, who contributed photos of Dave Cowens and Boston's world championship efforts in 1974 and '76.

Once again, many thanks are in order for this edition of the *Greenbook*. First to Tod Rosensweig, the Celtics' vice president for communications, who edited and supervised the project. And to David Zuccaro, the Celtics' director of publications and information, who authored the player bios and compiled the statistics in the back matter and who served as copy editor. Also vital was my editor, Tim Orwig, who understands writing better than anyone I know. Plus Jeff Twiss, the Celtics' public relations director, and Wayne Levy, the assistant in public relations, were more than gracious in making sure materials and information were available.

The staff at Taylor Publishing Company did much of the yeoman's work in pushing the *Greenbook* along. And my wife, Karen Snidow Lazenby, spent long hours seeing the book through the stages of electronic publishing.

Beyond that, the New England newspapers again supplied their excellent coverage of the team. The list of the best should include Peter May, Jackie MacMullan and Bob Ryan at the *Globe*. They were excellent, as were Steve Bulpett and Mark Murphy at the *Herald*, and Jim Fenton at the *Brockton Enterprise* and Mike Fine of the *Quincy Patriot Ledger*. Their writing and reporting make Bostonians the best-informed basketball fans in America.

The list of those granting interviews begins with Celtics' president Red Auerbach, who took the time to discuss events as he saw them. Others who graciously agreed to be interviewed were Chris Ford, Jan Volk, Bob Cousy, Dave Cowens, Rick Barry, Ed Pinckney, Larry Bird, Robert Parish, Kevin McHale, Joe Kleine, A.J. Wynder, Reggie Lewis, Don Casey, Jon Jennings, Kevin Gamble, Dee Brown and Michael Smith.

Extensive use was made of a variety of publications, including *The National*, *The New York Times*, *Sports Illustrated*, *The Sporting News*, *Street & Smith's Pro Basketball Yearbook*, *USA Today* and *The Washington Post*.

The reporting work of a variety of writers helped tremendously: Jack Madden, Ted Green, Pat Putnam, Sandy Padwe, Jack McCallum, Sam Goldaper, Peter Vecsey, Alex Wolff and Bruce Newman.

Also, several books were key in my research, including: *Basketball for the Player, the Fan and the Coach* by Red Auerbach; *College Basketball's 25 Greatest Teams* by Billy Packer and Roland Lazenby; *Cousy on the Celtic Mystique* by Bob Cousy and Bob Ryan; *The Boston Celtics* by Bob Ryan; *The Modern Basketball Encyclopedia* by Zander Hollander; *The Official NBA Basketball Encyclopedia*, edited by Zander Hollander and Alex Sachare; and *Rick Barry's Pro Basketball Scouting Report* by Rick Barry and Jordan E. Cohn.

Roland Lazenby

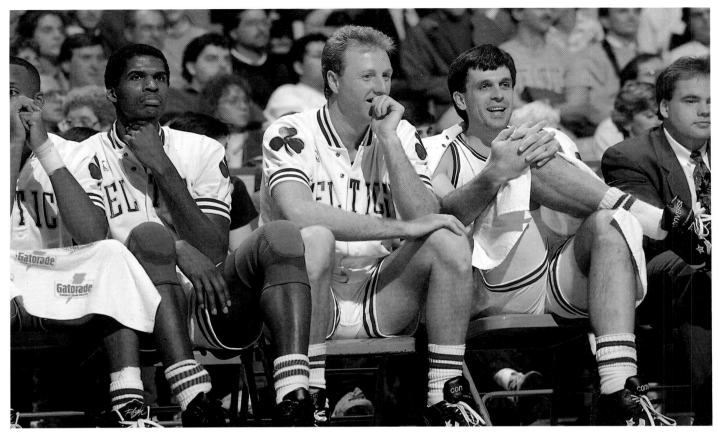

The view from the bench.

Battling L.A. in the '80s.

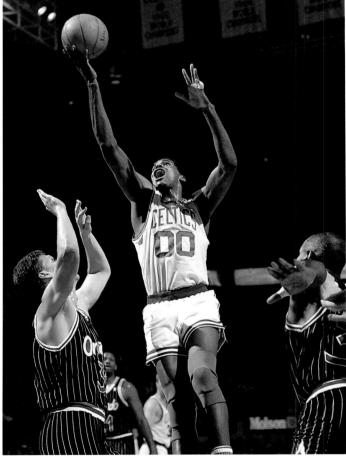

Stand back.

The post moves.

Three's Company

L arry. Kevin. Robert.
Bland as those three names are, they don't require much of an introduction around the NBA. Instead, they've acquired their own collective nickname—The Big Three. For the past 11 seasons, they've performed roundball miracles on the Garden parquet together. It's been a thrilling time for Boston crowds, who have spent the best months of each year watching Bird, Parish and McHale put together sequence after sequence of spectacular plays. The spectacular, in fact, has become almost commonplace. Meanwhile, the famed frontcourt has run up some astounding totals.

Like 60,017 points.

With 28,371 rebounds.

And 9,872 assists.

Plus 4,380 blocked shots and 3,020 steals.

All of which equals 722 wins, eight divisional titles, five conference championships and three NBA trophies.

If those numbers alone don't say enough, then Celtics' President Red Auerbach will be happy to chip in his two cents.

The passer.

The warrior.

Larry, Robert and Kevin have been together for nearly a fourth of the NBA's entire history.

"They are the greatest front line since the NBA was formed," Red says between puffs of his cigar.

Better than Mikan, Mikkelsen and Pollard.

Better than Reed, DeBusschere and Bradley.

Better than Kareem, Worthy and Green.

Better than Russell, Heinsohn and Ramsey.

Better than Cowens, Havlicek and Silas.

Better than Erving, Malone and Jones.

Better than Walton, Lucas and Gross.

Better than Pettit, Macauley and Hagan.

And certainly better than Laimbeer, Rodman and Edwards.

Asked to come up with a frontcourt to match The Big Three, TBS analyst (and Hall of Famer) Rick Barry suggested the 1967 Philadelphia trio of Wilt Chamberlain, Lucious Jackson and Billy Cunningham.

"That would be the only frontcourt that could come close to comparing to them," he said.

But even they couldn't matchup with the Celtics, Barry added.

Besides, Wilt, Jackson and Cunningham only played together two full seasons.

Larry, Robert and Kevin have been together for nearly a fourth of the NBA's entire history.

"That's obviously been smart on the Celtics' part," Barry said, "because they've kept the team extremely competitive."

It has also given the team a wonderful continuity. That became apparent last season when four young players—Brian Shaw, Reggie Lewis, Dee Brown and Kevin Gamble—teamed with the frontcourt

The mix of young and old.

to give the Celtics a splendid blend of quickness and experience. The young players got confidence out of the deal. The Big Three got a jolt of rejuvenation, which, frankly, they needed after 11 years and 60,000 points.

"You make a play that you made a zillion times before," McHale said, "and all of a sudden you have guys out there slapping five with each other. They bring a bit of enthusiasm to what we're doing. I see Dee, and he's out there slapping my hand.

"You see them, and it's the look in their eyes."

What the younger players give the Big Three in enthusiasm, they get

back in guidance and wisdom. "Those guys have been steady for 11 years," Brown said last spring. "You know you can count on them night in and night out. . . Those guys have gone through everything you can go through, they've been through so much and found every which way to win. We're learning about poise from them. It's good when they say, 'Let's be cool.'"

"The Big Three, we and everyone else realize what they give us," agreed Shaw. "They're going to be consistent. They're going to be constant. . . They definitely push you to a higher level. The type of effort they give, their intensity on the court,

Chief strides to the hole.

Controlling the defensive boards.

Doing battle does not come naturally to Robert Parish. He has willed himself a warrior. It is something he has learned and relearned night in and night out over those 1,345 NBA games.

there's no way you can give less than them. Besides, they won't let you."

THE SELF-MADE WARRIOR

His simple cordiality is part of the ritual. When it's game time, Robert Parish heads to center court and seeks out the opposition. He extends his hand for a quick touch and offers his slight trace of a smile. He gets more warmth out of this hint of a smile than most people get out of a full flash of teeth.

For 15 seasons, a total of 1,345 games, Parish has offered this sportsmanship before doing battle. It comes naturally to him. His family and breeding have made him a gentleman, albeit a quiet one. The battling, on the other hand, hasn't been so easy. Other players around

Robert still runs the floor like a youngster.

Sixteen years in the post.

"He's probabley the best medium-range shooting big man in the history of the game," former teammate Bill Walton said of Parish.

The Chief is adored in Boston.

the league often refer to Parish as a warrior, which befits his nickname.

He is, after all, the Chief.

He is paradoxically majestic.

But doing battle does not come naturally to Robert Parish. He has willed himself a warrior. It is something he has learned and relearned night in and night out over those 1,345 NBA games.

"They don't push him around," said Auerbach, one of Parish's biggest fans. "But he doesn't instigate much, either."

For someone who isn't a natural fighter, Parish has won his share of battles. At the same time, he has managed to win the war, too.

"Now I've grown into it," he said last year of the nickname (from Chief Bromden in the movie *"One Flew Over The Cuckoo's Nest"*). "I've developed the personality to go with the title."

In his own quiet, steady way, he has stamped this persona on pro basketball. There have been better NBA centers. But not too many. Russell was better. And Kareem. Wilt was better, too. But even those greats would have trouble matching Parish's consistency of performance.

Year in, year out, he has given the Celtics just what they have needed in the post.

"I'm a very competitive person," he explains. "If I wasn't, I wouldn't be here."

Consider that last season, at age 37, he was second in the league in rebounds per minute behind Houston's Hakeem Olajuwon. He also finished second in the league in field-goal percentage at .598, a career-high, as was his free-throw percentage, .767. Beyond that, he played in 81 regular-season games, his highest total since 1985-86.

In February, when the Celtics needed a strong showing for their first major western road trip, the Chief answered the call. In five games, he scored 95 points and had 62 rebounds. Boosted by his effort, Boston rang up a 4-1 record over the outing. Parish scored 29 in a win over the Lakers at the Forum, (including 21 in the first quarter) then had 20 rebounds in Phoenix four nights later.

You would think that all that effort and travel would have tired out the league's oldest player. But he returned to the Garden on February 22 and pitched in another 26 points and 17 rebounds in a win over New Jersey.

This outburst fairly thrilled observers, and *Sports Illustrated* promptly celebrated by making him the cover of its March 11 issue.

"After 11 seasons in Boston," wrote SI's Alex Wolff, "under four coaches, through three championships—only George Mikan, Bill Russell and Kareem Abdul-Jabbar have played center for as many title teams—Parish is quietly, proudly and inexorably still there."

No one was more pleased by all of this than Dallas Mavericks' assistant coach Clifford Ray, who has witnessed firsthand this making of a warrior.

"He's my best friend," he declares proudly whenever asked about Parish.

Ray was the grizzled veteran center for the Golden State Warriors in 1976 when Parish broke in as a shy, uncertain first-round draft pick out of Centenary. The Warriors were a highly regarded team then, having

Bird's back is again a key question.

won the league championship a year earlier.

Ray says Parish was a gifted, but easily intimidated rookie who obviously needed some guidance. Ray took the time to help, and 15 years later he still gets excited watching Parish play.

"When I looked at him years and years ago, I knew he was gonna be great," Ray said. "I used to tell the Warrior front office, 'I'm gonna bring this kid along. He's gonna be a great player.'"

The Warriors, though, didn't see what Ray saw.

"He always had great offensive ability," Ray said of Parish. "But he did not feel confident in his game as a rebounder and defender. That was just hard work, but he had never really pushed himself. He used to say to me, 'Clifford, if I had your drive, I could be great.'

"I said, 'I'm gonna give you that drive. You're gonna be great. You gotta believe that what you're going

through now is just an adjustment that every young player makes. I'm beating you now. But one day I'm going to be sitting in the stands watching you play. And I'm gonna be enjoying it. I'm gonna smile every time I see you, because all those people who thought I was an idiot will realize that I knew what I was talking about.'"

Unfortunately for the Warriors, they didn't listen to Ray. They decided instead to trade Parish to Boston along with a first-round draft pick that Auerbach would use to select McHale. Golden State then used those picks to select Joe Barry Carroll and Rickey Brown.

"I don't think they used Robert right," Auerbach said of the Warriors. "We saw his talent and figured that through proper coaching and so forth that he could be good."

But even Red had no idea that Parish would just keep getting better year after year. "Most players age differently," observed Auerbach, who at 74 has become something of an

expert on the aging process. "For example, Havlicek [who left the game in 1978 after playing 16 years] aged mentally. He could have played much longer. It was the same with Sam Jones, Cousy and Russell. They all could have played longer. But they'd sort of *had* it."

Parish, on the other hand, seems quite content to keep getting it. "Mentally and physically, he's quite a guy at taking care of himself," Auerbach said. "Some players get old early. They have trouble with weight problems and off-season conditioning."

Not Parish. A few years back, he began to feel his age when training camp opened, so he decided to give up alcohol and to train year round. Like his conservative investments, the time spent working on his body has paid off. ("A body like that comes along once a century," observed Chicago Bulls general manager Jerry Krause.) His $2-million-plus annual contract is a big part of the motivation to keep playing,

Larry gave Chuck a hand during the playoffs.

is, if it was possible, he'd do it [fulfill the contract]."

To help that happen, the Celtics "tried to cut his minutes a little bit." That helped save the wear and tear, and now Parish seems ready for his 16th season, which, if he keeps progressing as he has the past few years, could be his sweetest.

BACK IN ACTION?

"It's incredible," Dee Brown said after Larry Bird's big performance against Charlotte last November. "The guy scores 45 points, and he has eight assists, too. I hope people don't overlook the eight assists."

It's quite possible that no one ever overlooks anything that Larry Bird does. After all, he is, as the sports media have taken to calling him, "Larry Legend."

He is an American icon.

It's a tough role to play, particularly in your advancing years, but if his back is healed from off-season surgery, this icon will embark on his 13th NBA season in the fall of 1991. He will turn 35 on December 7. Even the New England Optimists' Club would hedge on the Celtics' odds of having him in uniform when the campaign opens.

As Red Auerbach said in July, no one really knows if Bird can come back from this latest round of surgery. Not even his doctors know for sure.

"If anyone can do it, he can," Red said, "because he's got a high tolerance for pain. Right now, he's got no pain. He's walking six to seven miles a day and exercising and doing lots of things. So far, it's good. But you don't know what's going to happen when he starts jumping and jarring it."

The indications, however, seemed positive a few days after his June 7 surgery to relieve pain from an inflamed bone and swollen disc in his back.

"People said back surgery should be a last resort, not to have it," Bird said. "All I know is I had pain all last year and I couldn't move very well. Right now, I feel 100 percent and have no pain whatsoever."

Auerbach said. "The main thing about Robert is his personality. He's coachable. He does what he's asked. He's the consummate pro."

Parish credits much of his approach to Ray, who preached consistency to him. He also helped him understand his role. "A center's got to look at one thing—the outcome of the game," Ray once told him. "Did we win? Win often enough, and people will say you're the reason why. You're always going to have stars, you're always going to have colorful players. But you can't win without someone who rebounds and plays defense and brings people together."

While Bird and McHale have gotten most of the attention, Parish has quietly lived up to the ideals that Ray instilled in him. He became a

rebounder and a defender, and his offensive skills have only grown sweeter in Boston, where the fans ooh and aah over his arched shots. "He's probably the best medium-range shooting big man in the history of the game," former teammate Bill Walton told SI.

And because of all those things, the Celtics were more than willing to sign him to a $5.5-million, two-year contract extension at age 36, a time when most players are already making Miller Lite commercials.

The team brass made the decision on the contract with little anxiety, Auerbach said, and they were willing to do it for two reasons:

1) "It's very hard to get another center. There aren't many of them out there today."

2) "Knowing the type of person he

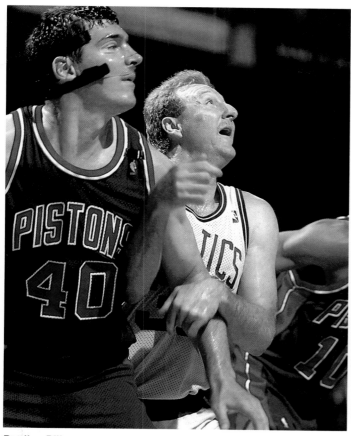

Battling Bill.

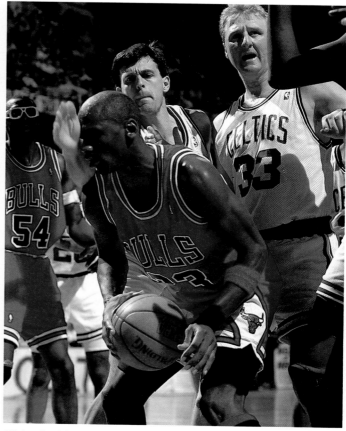

Mixing it with Mike.

Bird went to the parquet in Game 5 against the Pacers.

Larry greets Jordan before their March showdown.

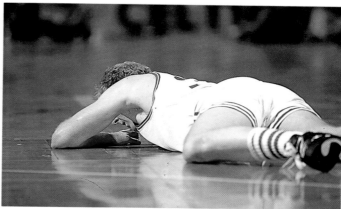

A few weeks later, he felt well enough to joke about missing his usual summer routine. "Not being able to play golf is costing me a lot of money," he said with characteristic deadpan. "But right now I'd be happy just to walk around the course and drink beer."

Turning more serious, he said, "I don't know how long it will be until I can run, or play golf, or shoot a basketball. But it might be three months. . . That's how long I'll be in this brace."

The caution in his voice is understandable, considering his previous experience with injury and surgery. He has had to make quite an adjustment since returning from bone-spur surgery on both of his heels in 1989. It hasn't been easy. In the mid 1980s, he was clearly the game's best player. But injuries and the aging process have changed that now. As Celtics' radio man Glenn Ordway explained, Bird is merely one of the top 15 or so players in the game.

"I guess that's a fact," Boston center Joe Kleine quipped last season. "Nobody ever stays at the same level forever. For five, six, seven, eight years in a row, he was the best player in the world. Now he's only an All-Star. I feel really bad for him, don't you?"

Kleine's humor aside, there were legions of fans disturbed that his surgery and painful recovery reduced Bird's effectiveness. Now, however, those same fans are merely hoping that he'll be able to continue his playing career, and that if he does continue, his game won't change.

Bird, meanwhile, freely admits that the game has changed for him. "Even now, I'm not close to what I used to be," he said last season. "I feel pretty good, but I don't think there's any question that I haven't put it together like I did before the surgeries. But that's part of it. I had some major surgery, and I have to live with what I got."

From Joe Kleine's perspective that may not seem like such a terrible thing. Bird, though, is used to much more.

"The most frustrating thing is to

Bird didn't lose the quickness he never had.

play when you're not able to play at 100 percent every night," he told the *Boston Globe's* Jackie MacMullan last season. "Even now I'm not close to being the way I used to be. My confidence just isn't where it once was, and it probably never will be again. I thought last year [1989-90] I could get it all back, but it never happened."

The change forced Bird to accept a new role with the team. It wasn't easy, he said. "I'm not involved in every play anymore. I don't handle the ball in every situation the way I used to. Back when I was playing with M.L. [Carr] and Max [Cedric Maxwell], when the going got tough, I knew the ball was coming to me every time. I knew the picks would be set a little better, and the ball would be thrown into my hands right where I needed it.

"But now we have a new team. We have a lot of guys that came from different situations who have never won. Most of these guys have never been in a situation where they won night in and night out.

"I knew there would be a time when someone else would be ready to step forward, to get things done. I can accept that. What matters is winning."

The greatest front line in NBA history.

McHale with Dave Gavitt and Havlicek.

At the start of last season, Bird shifted from small to power forward, which meant he played closer to the basket. Early in the schedule, he was noticeably absent taking three-point shots. But within weeks he had adjusted and was again firing up treys.

There had been questions about his ability to fit into Chris Ford's new running game, but those questions rapidly disappeared. Throughout his career, Bird has been an excellent defensive rebounder and outlet passer. Surgery hadn't altered those skills, so more often than not, he was feeding Boston's new break.

"On the defensive boards, as soon as I get the ball, I pass it to Brian," Bird explained. "While he's pushing it up I see everything that's going on while I'm running. By the time he gets ready to make his decisions, unless he's got a guy breaking for a layup, I'll be around the free-throw line, waiting."

If the good shot opened quickly on the break, the Celtics took it. If not,

the ball went to Bird, and they ran their offense.

When the Celtics pulled up to play the half-court game, he was deadly. He would be poised on the perimeter, holding the ball with both hands up over his right shoulder, posing a shooting threat. Defenses were forced to come out and play him, which then opened up the floor, making his passing skills all the more deadly.

It translated into a beautiful November and December, the kind of opening that made Bostonians fall in love with basketball all over again. Even a grizzled observer like the Globe's Bob Ryan had a new spring in his step. With guard Dee Brown proving to be an incredible find as a rookie and Brian Shaw providing just what was needed at the point, the Celtics were something to behold. Bird tended to run a bit hot and cold in his shooting, but that didn't matter. "The last guy on the team I worry about is Larry," McHale said. "He's playing excellent defense. He's

rebounding well, passing well. He may not be stroking the ball like he once did, but he's doing the other things."

Mainly, the young players fed off his boundless confidence. Kevin Gamble filled the hole nicely at small forward. Shaw and Reggie Lewis were the backcourt, while Parish and Bird started up front. Off the bench came McHale and Brown. Bird sensed something special was happening.

"I like this team," he admitted.

They all did. "It's like being traded, like a new life," Parish said of the Celtics' new look. "To see our young guys so gung-ho is great. The backcourt is where people had been breaking us down, which put more pressure on me and Kevin defensively. If we didn't do something about our backcourt, we were in for another long year, and nobody wanted that.

"Brian, Reggie, Dee, Gamble—all of these guys are looking to push it up the floor and making us older guys run, which is good," he continued. "It's gonna create a lot of easy baskets, which saves the wear and tear on us older guys. Plus it puts pressure on the other team's defense."

Suddenly, foes around the league began to realize that reports of Bird's demise were exaggerated. "They say he's a step slower," Philadelphia's Fred Carter confided to Ryan, "but his game hasn't changed any. He's still got great eyes and great hands, and he's able to do all the things he's

"I'm no slower than I was 10 years ago," Bird said. "I've got compensating down to a science."

been doing. His game never was built on speed."

Bird agreed.

"I'm no slower than I was 10 years ago—though that's not saying much, is it?" he said to *Boston Herald* columnist Joe Fitzgerald.

Much of his game had changed, but he also pointed out that much of his game was built to weather the years. "I've always had to use my body because I've never been able to compete with guys in the leaping department," he said of his rebounding. "Same with my offense. I've always been the type of player who had to look for shortcuts coming up the floor, trying to keep up, trying to figure the game to where I could take that shortcut and still guard my man. Heck, I've spent my whole career trying to make up for my lack of quickness.

"I'm no slower than I was 10 years ago," he said. "I've got compensating down to a science."

Also remaining intact was his nose for success. "I've been doing this since I was a kid," he said. "I've been playing basketball every day of my life, and the one thing I've always been taught is win, win, win. I felt that way at 15, and I felt that way at 30.

A chat with Cousy.

So what's a few more years?

"My intensity level's the same as it's always been."

Since coming back from heel surgery and finding that his shooting touch had become a bit tentative, he had struggled with his confidence. But the winning helped take care of that. They closed November on an eight-game winning streak to finish the month at 12-2.

Better yet, on November 30, in a blowout of the Washington Bullets in Boston Garden, he scored his 20,000th point, making him one of just five players, including Havlicek, Abdul-Jabbar, Oscar Robertson and Jerry West, to record 20,000 points

and 5,000 assists in an NBA career.

Bird recorded his 20,000th point on a 17-foot jumper with about eight minutes left in the third period.

"It's not really that big a deal," he said afterward. "It's a lot of jumpers in a lot of guys' faces.

"If they paid us by the point, I'd have 50,000 by now."

Ford, however, disagreed: "That's a tremendous achievement. Not only to score yourself, but to get 5,000 assists. Larry has a tremendous will to succeed. Whatever it takes, he works at it. And he enjoys helping his teammates as well."

Bird said he thought of Dennis Johnson when he hit the bucket. "I

The Chief gets hailed.

was around DJ a long time," he said, "and he always said assists mean more than points. Five thousand assists is good."

With the momentum of that milestone, Bird and the Celtics found December to be just as good. He scored 43 with 13 assists in a win over the Nuggets. "I hate to say it," said Denver coach Paul Westhead, "but I almost enjoy watching him. He does it with such delightful pleasure."

On December 19 against Philly, Bird had 24 points, eight assists, seven rebounds and six steals. He was thriving. "I've got a different role, and I enjoy playing it," he told the *Quincy Patriot-Ledger's* Mike Fine. "Doing the same things you've been doing for 11 years can get a little old. This league can get to you. You're playing against the same people. Like when you play against Atlanta 57 times... which I've done. You just do the same things over and over again."

The mix of young guards and forwards was changing all that, he said.

Bolstered by another nine-game winning streak, they finished the month at 12-3 and were the talk of the league. They opened January the same way, with six straight wins, and by the morning of the 11th had the best record in the NBA at 30-5.

But the run was already over. An inflamed nerve in Larry's back had left him wracked with pain. Actually, the first sign of trouble had come in the exhibition season, when he missed a road trip to Buffalo and Toronto. For the first two months of the regular season, he played despite the pain. By January that was no longer possible.

With him out of the lineup, the Celtics suffered. He missed 14 games before the All-Star break and had to withdraw from the game in Charlotte. His back trouble dogged him the rest of the way. He missed 22 games over the schedule and barely made it back for the playoffs.

He still mustered the strength to turn in another legendary performance against the Indiana Pacers in the first round. Bird's face slammed into the Garden parquet

The Celtic frontcourt is loaded.

while he was going for a loose ball in the fifth and deciding game. He retreated to the locker room and was apparently out with a concussion. But his reappearance late in the game brought the Garden crowd alive as the Celtics held off the Pacers and Chuck Person.

The conference semifinals against Detroit were another matter. The pain and wear and tear had become too much, and Boston fell, four games to two. Obviously hurting, Bird still drew the admiration of observers. "Even during the playoffs, when he was operating at 40 percent, some teams were still playing two men on him," Celtics' TV analyst Bob Cousy pointed out. "You couldn't leave him alone. His confidence is supreme. He could be out there on one leg and still think he could hit the next six three-pointers in a row."

If nothing else, last season revealed that Boston's mix of old and new had much promise. A healthy and spirited Larry Bird can't provide all the answers for 1991-92. But the

Celtics are hoping that he can provide just enough. Then maybe they can rework their magic of last November and December into a similar show in May and June of 1992.

THE IRON RANGER

Kevin Edward McHale was raised in the northern Minnesota hamlet of Hibbing, not far from the Canadian border. The region is known as the Iron Range because of the ore that is mined there. Accordingly, the hearty people who work in the industry are known as Iron Rangers.

Kevin's father, Paul, worked as an Iron Ranger for 42 years before retiring in 1982.

That same work ethic has made Kevin a vital part of the Celtics' success for the past 11 years. During that time, he has done whatever the job required. He has played hurt. For his first 4 1/2 seasons, he put aside the ego satisfaction of a starting role to serve as a sixth man. He has played defense and blocked shots.

And he's been reasonably happy about operating in Larry Bird's substantial shadow.

Beyond that, as the Celtics have attempted to rebuild the last few seasons, he has even offered to be traded if it would make the team better.

That, of course, is an idea that Celtics' management has always nixed, and with good reason.

"Kevin is not replaceable," Bird told the Globe's Peter May in the summer of 1990. "Night in and night out, there is nobody in the NBA who can do the things he can do. There's just nobody out there coming in who can do those things. You don't trade a guy like Kevin for a couple of guys who might be able to help you. If Kevin was coming out this year, at his age, he'd still be the number-one pick. You wouldn't trade him for three picks, number one, two and three. There's just no way."

McHale is probably the best power forward in the history of the game, TBS analyst Rick Barry said recently.

That's a point on which most NBA general managers would agree. For years now, the 6'10" McHale, sporting a combination of 40-inch arms and squiggly post moves, has been considered nearly unstoppable. His career .562 field goal percentage attests to it. He has spent years perfecting his turnaround jumper and his muti-faceted short hook. From those two basics, he has fashioned an arsenal of moves, which he sets up with an array of fakes.

Between 1986 and 1988, he absolutely dominated basketball, leading the NBA two years running with a .604 field goal percentage. In 1986-87, he became the only player in league history to average better than 60 percent from the field and 80 percent from the line.

He's understandably proud of what he's accomplished. "Those two shots are awfully tough to stop," he said in 1988, "so what a guy has to do is take chances before I even shoot, which allows me to do other things."

The last two seasons he has expanded that weaponry to include the three-point shot. In the first nine years of his career, McHale made but 2 of 26 trey attempts. But in 1989-90, he took 69 three-pointers during the regular season and made 23, a solid .333. Last season, his attempts dropped to 37, but he made 15 of them, a whopping .405 average. Then in the playoffs, he went ballistic, shooting .545 from long range, making 6 of 11 attempts.

The past two seasons have also brought a return to his role as sixth man, a move that McHale was eager to make, partly because of his effectiveness from the bench early in his career. "I actually liked coming off the bench," he recalled. "I got to watch the flow of the game develop, and I felt real comfortable going in there and doing what I felt needed to be done to help the team."

As Frank Ramsey and John Havlicek had done before him, McHale thrived in that role, earning the league's Sixth Man Award in 1984 and '85. Now that he has returned to it, his value to the team has jumped yet again. His versatility provides the

The game is fun for McHale.

23

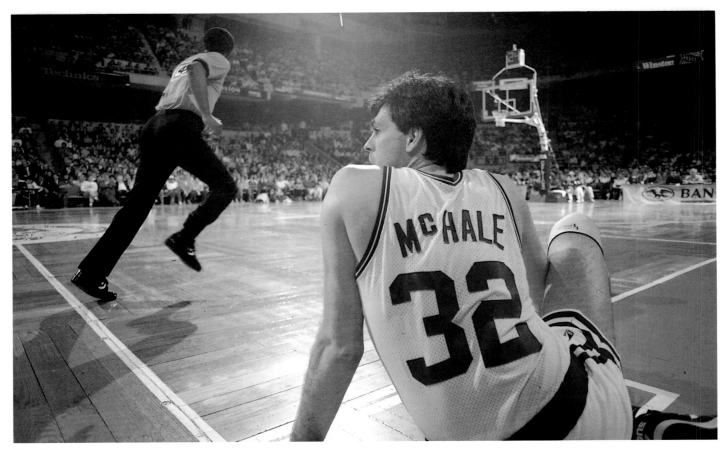

The sixth man.

frontcourt with great flexibility. He can join Parish and Bird in the lineup to make Boston very big across the front, or he can replace Parish to give the Celtics a smaller, quicker set. His ability to play center has helped Parish cut his minutes and remain more effective.

This versatility was a big reason for Boston's success last November and December. "We can go a lot of different lineups," Bird said at the time. "McHale plays center a lot this year. We can go small at time; we can go large. We can give 'em a lot of different looks, and that's really helped us."

Boston's newly constructed running game also worked to rejuvenate him. "It's a fun way to play the game," he said at the All-Star break.

And that, McHale insists, is what he's seeking in the later years of his career. It's what he has always sought.

The most fun, of course, is to win. And The Big Three would like nothing better than to add a fourth

Kevin keeps playing through the pain and soreness.

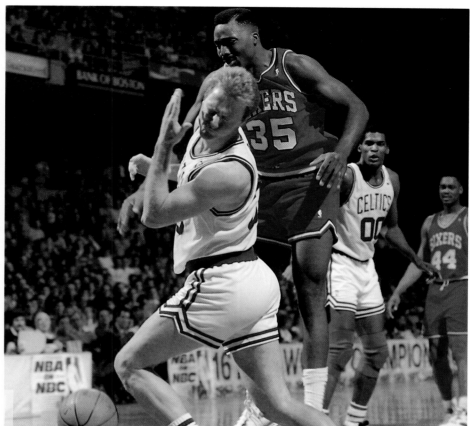

An Armon Larry?

championship. That's why they grind on past the pain, hoping to put it together for one more big run. Like Bird, McHale also played with injury last year, ligament damage in his left ankle. He had outpatient surgery in July and once again projected that he'd be ready for another campaign by training camp.

Robert. Kevin. Larry.

Certainly the most amazing thing about the Three is that they've achieved so much together. Usually, the downfall of a talented NBA frontcourt is that one ball simply isn't enough for three players. If there is a secret formula underneath their success, it's a fundamental unselfishness in all three. They haven't always been perfect and haven't always seen completely eye to eye. But most of the time they have played together and found strength in their numbers.

"It's whoever has the best shot, whoever's playing well, " McHale once explained to Globe reporter Ian Thomsen. "When you're in sync, it just happens. That's why, if you have two or three or four good players, you're a better team, because you can diversify your offense."

The only remaining question for

Dancin' with Dennis.

these three to answer is, how long will they run?

"I look at players that play way past their prime, and all of a sudden the game turns on you like a bad lover," McHale said in 1988. "All of a sudden it's not so good for you. Things aren't working the way they should. God gave me the ability to play, He blessed me in so many ways, and I want to go out with the attitude that rather than struggle to play another year or so you can get another contract when you're way past your prime and just kind of holding on."

"We all know," Parish said at the 1991 All-Star break, "that our days are winding down."

Which only makes the upcoming season all the more special. Parish and Bird are both in the final year of contracts. And while McHale has signed a new two-year contract, he has made it known that he'll quit when the game's no longer fun.

"I'll probably retire one night in Cleveland," he said a few years

Usually, the downfall of a talented NBA frontcourt is that one ball simply isn't enough for three players. If there is a secret formula underneath their success, it's a fundamental unselfishness in all three.

A Bird Christmas
(As told to Joe Fitzgerald of the *Boston Herald*)

"You know how they say it was the grinch who stole Christmas? It wasn't the grinch at all. It was the rich people. They're the ones who've stolen it, who've put a price tag on it, buying everything they can for their kids and not worrying about other kids who are going to end up feeling left out. They've taken Christmas the wrong way. It's supposed to be a time for letting people know how you feel about them, isn't it?

"But what kills me is that while Christmas is a time of excitement for some people, it's a time that makes a lot of other people sad, like kids who just can't have the things they see their friends getting. A lot of people—and I know people like this—just can't wait for Christmas to be gone.

"...whenever I'm with a bunch of kids I always look for that one kid who stands off by himself, whose clothes don't look too good. I'll go out of my way to make a big deal over him, because I used to be that kid.

"Once when I was in the seventh grade, a bank bought tickets for us to go watch the Pacers play the Kentucky Colonels. Our coaches took us, and I can remember my mom giving me a dollar. All the other kids were buying souvenir basketballs, autographed pictures, pennants, everything, and all I had was that dollar for a Coke. I remember being embarrassed because I wasn't able to buy anything. But you know what? I look back at that now and, yeah, it was sad, but in a way being poor was the best thing that ever happened to me, 'cause it's made me appreciate all I have today.

"We got mostly clothes, 'cause that's what we needed. I can remember my friends getting bicycles, and me thinking how I'd buy the best bike in town if only I had the money. But that just wasn't possible. Still, my mom did a good job. Christmas was a big thing around our house. There was always a pile of five or six gifts for all of us. As soon as you opened one, you went right to the next one. It was chaos, and even though we knew it wasn't going to be a lot, we knew how tough it was for them to get us what they did. But sometimes she'd surprise us. Once I got a watch.

".... tell all those kids who didn't get what they wanted that Larry Bird sends a special Merry Christmas! to them. Tell them they may not understand it now, but they can take my word for it, if they've got people in their lives who love 'em, they're a whole lot richer than they think."

back. "It'll be snowy and rainy and crappy and we'll have lost to the Cadavers by like 40, and I'll probably say, 'That's it,' and go home."

That wouldn't be such a terrible ending, considering what they've accomplished.

On the other hand, it wouldn't be bad to close it as a storybook either. Noon at City Hall plaza in June with a clear blue Boston sky. With green and white balloons filling the horizon, and Red puffing and grinning while the biggest crowd in Beantown history roars as the Big Three thrust another trophy up for all to see.

They'll pause there, soaking in the noise and tumult and applause one final time, knowing their work is finished. The Chief, of course, will offer his trace of a smile, and that will be plenty bright enough.

The unstoppable post moves.

Ford is at home on the parquet.

Doctor, Doctor

Chris Ford, his arms folded, stands alertly at the sideline in Boston Garden. He barks an order at his players, then stops and shakes his head at something he sees. Kevin Gamble is at the free-throw line, and when he scores, Ford applauds politely with the Garden crowd. The action resumes, and Ford again burnishes the parquet with his gaze. Brian Shaw may be handling the ball, but Ford is the real point guard here, constantly shouting orders and directing traffic, offering approval, then snatching it back with a glare. The Celtics score and move back quickly on defense. Ford nods happily when they force a traveling call. He pumps three fingers in the air, calling out the offense as his team heads upcourt with the ball. As the action picks up, so does his chatter. To make sure his players hear him, Ford cups his hands around his face and shouts.

Yes, Chris Ford is like E.F. Hutton. His players listen.

"Chris tells you exactly what he wants," forward Ed Pinckney said. "If you don't do it, you get to sit on the bench and watch somebody else do it."

Celtics president Arnold "Red" Auerbach once remarked that former Boston coach Jimmy Rodgers simply hadn't been strong enough with this veteran Celtics team. But that isn't a problem with Chris Ford. In no uncertain terms, he has emerged as the team's tough boss, which just may be the biggest of the many surprises from the Celtics' 1990-91 season.

The players call him "Doc," his nickname from his playing days when he once boldly windmilled in the face of Doctor J. In Boston these days, it seems the Doctor is in. In charge.

In Boston these days, it seems the Doctor is in. In charge.

"I like everything Chris did last year," said Celtics TV analyst Bob Cousy. "He related to the players, but he maintained discipline, too. Considering all that, he might have done it as effectively as anyone since Arnold."

That is quite an accomplishment in the modern version of the NBA, Cousy says. In the old days, coaches had discipline, but today coaches have to "communicate" with their players or they don't last long. "Today the buzzword is communication," Cousy said. "Well, you know what that means. You say yes to everything the players ask. The minute Pat Riley tried to discipline his players, he was out in Los Angeles. I'm a traditionalist. I don't think the tail should be wagging the dog. But let's be realistic. Coaches are always

expendable. The owner can find 12 Red Auerbachs the next day. He can't find 12 Larry Birds."

Which means pro coaches today, in the age of long-term, guaranteed player contracts, have to use rhetoric to motivate, whereas Auerbach and other old-time pro coaches could resort to a little fear every now and then.

"Today pro coaching is a crap shoot," Cousy said.

And that is why Ford's success is so refreshing, he added. "His experience as a player has really paid off. He knew how to establish discipline—without being demonstrative about it. And that's the key. The players will accept it, if you don't flaunt it. Ford did it quietly, within the confines of the locker room."

Cousy, of course, has misspoken here. It hasn't always been quiet. There was the much-reported incident between Ford and Bird on the very first day of practice. Bird had made the mistake during a media interview of making light of Ford's plans to establish the running game. Ford read Bird's comments in the newspaper and arrived at Hellenic College for practice the next day loaded for bear.

He and Bird exchanged broadsides and expletives. When the smoke cleared, the team knew who was the boss.

"Everybody knew he was a tough guy," Pinckney said, "but when he laid down the law we really knew this was gonna be a no-nonsense guy. He wasn't gonna take a lot of crap from anybody—coaching staff, players, officials, anybody.

"From that first day, you knew that if you did not get things accomplished, you would not play.

"It was fresh."

Ford was relieved to see Shaw's return.

Brian Shaw also saw the incident as vital to the team's development. "Bird simply stated how things had been in the past," he recalled. "Chris stated what was gonna be happening now, that this wasn't the past anymore. It was understood how we were gonna play the game from that point on.

"They both gained a little respect, in my opinion," Shaw added. "Chris had to establish himself as a coach, and Larry said what he wanted to say. And that was it."

The incident remained unknown to the media until weeks later when USA Today's Peter Vecsey revealed it in a column. Even then, Ford had no comment about it.

"After we were finished blowin' smoke, we got together by ourselves for five minutes and settled the whole thing," Bird told Vecsey. "I told him, 'You tell me what to do, and I'll do it.

And there'll be no second-guessin'.'

"I always respected Chris. He's a good friend. I respect him even more now."

More important, so did the rest of the team. "Everything was established," Pinckney said. "This was the way we were gonna do things. We weren't gonna do things like last year."

"We needed that drill sergeant mentality going into training camp," Parish said. "I think Chris gave us that. He put his foot down and didn't take any crap from anybody."

That, after all, had been Ford's vow when he had taken over—that he was going to do things his way. "I know there are a lot of people looking over my shoulder, and there will always be a lot of questions," he said in November. "But I said I was going to do it the way I felt best. I realize that means you can either look

brilliant or really dumb."

The surprise in all of this is that as a Celtics' assistant coach for seven years, Ford seemed almost meek. "As an assistant, Chris had little to say," recalled Cousy. "He has turned out to be much sterner than any of us expected."

"One thing about assistant coaches who become head coaches, they change overnight," observed Bird.

Auerbach, however, expressed no surprise at Ford's transformation. "He always was a fierce competitor," the team president said. "He knows what it is to win. He likes to win, and he knows he has to do certain things to help the team."

And that, said Auerbach with satisfaction, is why he wanted Ford as coach.

Ford was a starter on the '81 title team.

OLD YELLER

"I thought he did a good job," Bird said of Ford after Boston's opening game against Cleveland last season. "But I wish we would find a muzzle for him. He just never shuts up."

"I thought he'd get thrown out of games all the time," Pinckney said, "because he yells a lot. He's very vocal."

While it appeared that Ford was headed toward setting a record for ejections, just the opposite happened. By the All-Star break he hadn't gotten so much as a technical. Instead, he had guided the Celtics to the best record in the Eastern Conference over the first half of the season, leading to his being named as the East's All-Star coach, only the fourth rookie coach in league history to earn

"I thought he'd get thrown out of games all the time," Pinckney said, "because he yells a lot. He's very vocal."

that distinction. Ed Macauley, Billy Cunningham and Pat Riley were the other three.

"It was something he thought would be a great honor, but not something he was striving for," Ford's wife Kathy confided to the *Boston Globe's* Jackie MacMullan. "I was the one lying awake at night. I can't tell you how calm he was. I'm losing sleep, and he was snoring."

Ejections or no, Ford had made

much use of his vocal style, as Globe columnist Bob Ryan pointed out to Dee Brown after a December game. "Do you hear Doc when he's yelling?" Ryan asked.

"Yeah, I hear him," Brown replied. "He's non-stop. When you're on the court, it goes in one ear. You filter out what you need. The rest goes out the other ear. It doesn't bother me at all. I look at it as constructive criticism. He's basically yelling at me about the things I'm not doing right. That's his coaching style. I don't mind it at all, really."

Asked about all this, Ford said of his sideline antics: "I like it because you let loose with the stress and it's easier than being confined to a seat. You walk the sidelines, let some frustration out. I feel good doing it. I apologize to all the fans whose view I obstruct. But not to the media."

About his yelling he said, "I don't think I'm overbearing."

His players agree.

"The players joke a lot with Coach Ford," said guard A.J. Wynder, who was brought up from the Continental Basketball Association last season. "But when it comes down to business, Coach Ford says whatever he has to say. People listen.

"He's tough when you're not doing what he asks you to do. He's very demanding. He wants you to play the pressure defense and push the ball up. Those are the main things he asks. Some coaches hold players back. They say, 'I'm the boss,' this and that. But Coach Ford let's you play. When you're not doing the defense, when you're not pushing the ball, when you're not concentrating and playing heady basketball, he's gonna be on you."

He uses the yelling to maintain team concentration, backup center Joe Kleine said. "I think he likes to yell and shout, to try to fire up guys by yelling at them."

Ford seems to distribute this noise equally, Kleine said. "If you need to be yelled at, he yells at you. But he's not out just to get in your throat. He does it to everybody. That's the thing we all like about it. He'll yell at the big guys as well as the guys who don't play much."

Ford rules timeouts.

Like college players, Ford's Celtics run the lines.

That tenacity seems to make Ford's players want to play for him. To them, he is much more that just another set of sideline lungs.

Even Auerbach left certain people alone. But when McHale failed to block out during an early game with Denver, Ford jumped on the veteran forward angrily during a timeout and hurled a clipboard. "When was the last time you saw a Celtic coach do that?" asked *Providence Journal* columnist Bill Reynolds.

While Ford doesn't hesitate to confront and push his veterans, he is also fiercely protective of them. When a Boston television station misconstrued a teammate's comment into a criticism of Bird's shooting last March, Ford angrily lashed out at what he thought was the media attempting to stir up trouble. Some observers thought the response was unwarranted, but Ford had moved quickly to mash the problem.

That tenacity seems to make Ford's players want to play for him. To them, he is much more than just another set of sideline lungs.

"Chris has been in the organization so long, he knows our strengths and weaknesses," McHale said late last season. "He knew what our capabilities were and knew what we needed to do to become a better team.

"He hasn't been stuck in the coaching mold so long that he does things out of habit. He's not just X's and O's. Being a former player he still does things out of instincts."

Parish agreed: "He's one of the few coaches I know who doesn't complicate a simple game."

"He's a players' coach," Wynder said. "He knows what it's all about, when they're feeling hurt and what they might be going through. He can look into the players and see just what they're gonna give him that day. At least it seems that way."

When he talks, they listen.

It's like this, Kleine said, "From the standpoint of having been a player, he can see a lot of things before they happen."

And although he forces the level of intensity, he seems to know when to back off and call on his sense of humor. "He uses it all the time," Pinckney said. "Sometimes he'll break right in the middle of a tense moment and come out with something really funny."

His sense of his players has allowed him to build a coalition. He gives as much as he demands. "He's been really fair to me throughout the year," Pinckney said during last year's playoffs. "He's given me a number of chances to jumpstart my

game and get it going. Throughout the year, when other people have gotten down on my game, he was always there to pick me up.

"He has his way of dealing with everybody. His way of pushing me is to yell at me. He yells all the time, on the floor and in practice. He wants me to succeed, so he's always trying. He's always prodding and prodding. He wants more productivity. He never lets me get a rest on the floor, so he's always pushing and pushing and pushing."

It seems that Ford's solution to many things is to run. In practice, if the players aren't working, Ford stops things and has them put away the balls and run the lines.

33

Mr. Style.

Blowup.

Ford yells at the vets, too.

Ford with son, Chris Jr.

They run and run. It helps establish a cameraderie among the players, Pinckney says. "Get rid of the balls and run the lines. You do that in college but you don't do it in the NBA. But that's what we do."

THE NEXT ROUND

Like any rookie who has had a great year, Chris Ford now faces the challenge of the sophomore slump. But he has already overcome the biggest challenge—establishing his authority.

With that out of the way, he is free to focus on another overwhelming task, dealing with the uncertainty of Bird's health. Replacing the game's greatest forward would be the kind of task that overwhelms most coaches. Ford, though, refuses to be dominated by the situation.

"Hey, the beat goes on. This is the NBA," he said last spring when asked about Bird's back. "Someone has to step up. To talk about him not playing doesn't cut the mustard. It's like a crutch. You've got a job to do, go out and do it."

Without Bird last spring, the Celtics drifted into mediocrity. His aggressiveness seems to drive much of their mentality. Not to mention what

Doc uses his sense of humor.

his defensive rebouding does for Ford's running game. With Bird out, opponents began swooping in for bunches of offensive boards, and the Celtics slowed to a grind.

If Bird comes back healthy, many of those problems will take care of themselves. If he doesn't, Ford will have to rely on his toughness to force the team's aggressiveness and to build his young players' confidence.

As for the defensive boards, he may have to take to quoting Pat Riley from a few years back.

"No rebounds, no rings."

Whatever his solution, Ford will have to lead the team out of its uncertainty.

The direction will begin with his personal confidence. To find that, his players need look no further than the sideline. He'll be there, burnishing the floor with that gaze and calling for more effort.

As Pinckney says, "He's always pushing and pushing and pushing."

Gamble is one of the best finishers in the league, Bird says.

The Swing Man

On November 15, 1990, Larry Bird scored 45 points against the Charlotte Hornets. Almost lost in the euphoria over Bird's explosion was Kevin Gamble's first start of the 1990-91 season.

He scored 26 points on 10-of-14 shooting from the floor.

For those of you who don't have a calculator handy, that's 70 percent accuracy. Plus he had nine assists.

Basketball secrets, of course, live short lives in Boston, and within hours of his big game the local stat rats were marveling over Gamble's performance.

From there, it seems, the story just kept getting better. Gamble, a Continental Basketball Association refugee, has spent most of his life persevering against substantial odds. Last season, his silent, low-key brand of determination paid off as he moved rather smoothly into the starting lineup. By the end of November he was averaging 12.4 points on 58-percent shooting. More important, the Celtics were 7-0 with him as a starter.

"Kevin has a nose for the hoop, and he pushes the ball well," Ford said. "That's what he does for us, and that's what we need."

His emergence was something of a surprise in Boston, mainly because Gamble had mysteriously disappeared after the end of the 1988-89 season, when he had almost single-handedly delivered the Celtics into the '89 playoffs. He had been called up from the CBA and signed as a free agent in December 1988. But his game appearances were infrequent until Dennis Johnson's injury led then-coach Jimmy Rodgers to thrust Gamble into the starting lineup. Gamble responded by averaging 22.8 points over six games, good enough to lift the Celtics

Gamble, a Continental Basketball Association refugee, has spent most of his life persevering against substantial odds.

to 42-40 on the season and the eighth Eastern Conference playoff spot.

But Gamble suffered a groin pull in the first playoff game against the Pistons and was lost for the series, which Detroit promptly swept. At the time, it seemed Gamble might figure into Boston's plans for the 1989-90 season. But the year came and went, and Gamble was used sparingly. With starting point guard Brian Shaw having gone to Italy, Rodgers spent most of the season shuffling from one system to another trying to cover the team's weakness at the point. Gamble was lost in the confusion, and although he averaged about 12 minutes of playing time in 71 games, he was used inconsistently. As a result, he averaged a mere 5.1 points

per game and figured that his days in Boston were numbered.

A free agent at the end of the season, he signed a one-year contract and hoped for the best, which as it turned out, was exactly what Ford offered him.

The new season would bring a new start, Ford promised. With Shaw back and rookie guard Dee Brown coming in, the Celtics now had the personnel to run, and they were going to do just that, Ford said.

That seemed reasonable to Gamble. His skills would shine in the full-court game, although he thought he would get most of his minutes as a backup at off guard. But Ford had been searching for a solution to the Celtics' hole at small forward. He had given Michael Smith and Ed Pinckney a shot at the slot. But the 6'5" Gamble proved to be the right guy for the opening. He fit perfectly on the wing in the Celtics' running game. He could pull up and hit the outside shot, or he could put the ball on the floor and find his way to the hoop.

"I've always been a swing man," he explained. "I've always been a decent outside shooter. But the jump shot is not always going to be there. You gotta create."

Gamble is a lefty, and that is of immense value in scoring inside in the NBA. Plus his release is quick, and his shot has plenty of arch. All of which allowed him to thrive in Ford's open-court system. "When we're running, that gives me a chance to get to the basket, to get some good looks at scoring," he said.

"Kevin is pretty smart," Larry Bird observed. "He knows if he passes the ball, then cuts, he'll probably get it back. He's probably one of the strongest finishers in the league."

Celtics observers waited for

"It's a matter of being patient and not taking bad shots," Gamble said. "It's the style we play here too."

Gamble to wake up from his November dream, but that didn't happen. Just before the All-Star break in February, he lit up the Knicks for 32 points in Madison Square Garden by hitting 16 of 20 from the floor. That game boosted his shooting percentage to 62.5 on the season, the highest in the league.

Remarkably, he held close to that pace over the remainder of the schedule, finishing the season with a 15.6 scoring average and a .587 field goal percentage, third best in the league behind teammate Robert Parish and Portland's Buck Williams.

"It's a matter of being patient and not taking bad shots," Gamble told Jim Fenton of the *Brockton Enterprise*. "It's the style we play here, too. The players I play with make my game so easy. There are so many shot opportunities, and they come in easy situations. Larry, Robert and Kevin are such great passers."

To Gamble's credit, he recognized the opportunities the situation presented and then delivered what was required. He knew how to play with Boston's veterans.

"It's amazing what a little playing time will do," observed Parish.

"He feeds the post and then cuts off it so well," McHale said. "He cuts with a purpose in mind."

In many games, Gamble got off to a quick start, which was something the team needed. It also kept Gamble's confidence at a scoring level. His entire performance reflected a growing sense of maturity. He will turn 26 as the 1991-92 schedule opens. "I'm more at ease," he said last year. "This is really my third year and by now I know what I can and what I can't do."

That maturity has helped him

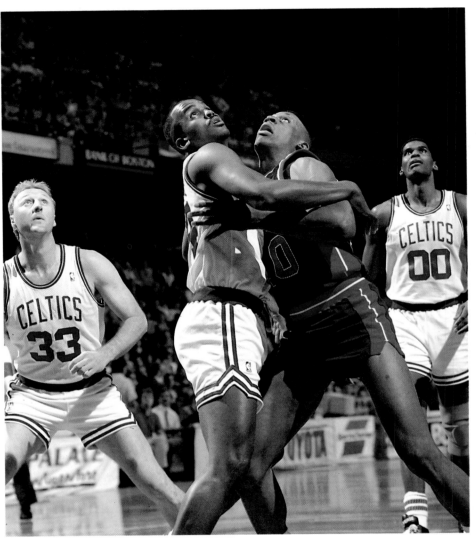

Gamble works at matching up.

understand his role in Boston. He gives the Celtics firepower and speed against the league's smaller lineups. And when they face big, powerful front lines, Gamble is accustomed to spending more time on the bench. "The problem comes when you go up against bigger teams with the matchups down low," Gamble admitted.

"I feel I'm a pretty good defender," he added. "Where I have my problems is on the pick and roll. That can be tough. But when I'm straight up on someone, I feel I'm a good defender."

Without question, he struggled during last year's playoffs. Over 11 games, his shooting percentage fell to .483 and he averaged just six points a game. Part of the drop-off could be attributed to playoff

basketball. Teams don't run as much, and the focus becomes the half-court matchups.

In that situation, Gamble seemed to lose some of his confidence, said Celtics TV analyst Bob Cousy. Is seems almost as if Gamble is still unsure of himself because of his CBA background, Cousy said. "He seems to be asking himself if he belongs in the NBA. Like a lot of young players who come in here, Gamble is an overachiever. The question always seems to be, 'Will they keep working after that initial success?' Last year, Ford had to use him, and he got his confidence early. The question now is, how is he gonna come out this year? Will he step up his game a level, or is he gonna revert? Only he can answer that."

Team president Red Auerbach

essentially agreed. "He fell off because they started concentrating on him," Auerbach said of Gamble's playoff performance, "and he didn't have enough weapons to counteract it. But if he thinks a lot about it and works on his game, he'll do fine."

Work has never been a problem for Kevin Gamble. The youngest of seven children, he grew up in the projects of Springfield, Illinois. All of the ghetto stereotypes apply here. The streets were mean. Plenty of guns and drugs. His father left the home when he was five. He could have been one of those statistics marching from childhood directly into the modern urban graveyard. But Gamble is different. He is deeply religious and carries with him a profound sense of right and wrong, much of it instilled by his mother.

As a result, he avoided trouble and became an all-stater at Lanphier High School. The summer after his senior season he was named MVP of the coaches' all-star game. But poor grades caught up with Gamble then. Instead of playing major college ball he went to Lincoln Junior College, which proved fortunate. There he was coached by Allen Pickering. A lot of coaches talk about being concerned about their players as people, but Pickering really meant it.

He insisted that his players study and develop academically. It was simple, Pickering told Gamble. If you want keep playing basketball, you have to make the grades to get to the next level. Gamble followed that plan, earning his associate's degree in two years while averaging 20.9 points

"He's a survivor," Pickering told the *Boston Globe's* Peter May. "At every level, he stuck it out. Those are the kinds of things you go through which make you the person you are. . . . Kevin never asked for anything. He tried to be just like everyone else. He never missed a practice. He did all the wind sprints."

He wanted to play Big 10 basketball at Illinois, but coach George Raveling at Iowa was more interested in him as a player. So Gamble went there and again played impressively. Dr. Tom Davis replaced

Breakway.

Kevin fits in with the vets.

and saw the talent, the guys were just as good as I was," he said. "I didn't give myself a timetable for getting back to the NBA. I felt I had played well enough in Portland that I would be called back. It just didn't happen right away."

In the offseason, he accepted an offer to play in the Phillipines, then came back and tried summer camps in Detroit and Charlotte without success. The start of the 1988-89 season found him back in the CBA at Quad City, where he again drew attention as a big scorer. He noted

The Hawkeyes rode Gamble's game through the '87 NCAA tournament until he got into foul trouble against Nevada-Las Vegas. Without him on the floor, they lost.

with some irony that pro scouts always preach about defensive concerns, but what draws them to CBA games is a big scorer.

He was leading the league in scoring when the Celtics came calling in December 1988. He had figured he would catch on with another NBA team, but he never thought it would be Boston. Sure enough, Danny Ainge made it official by giving him a nickname his first day of practice. Oscar. For the baseball player.

His ups and downs didn't end there, of course. But last season marked an arrival of sorts for Kevin Gamble. "It's a lot of fun starting in the NBA," he said. "You dream about things like that. Hopefully, this will continue for me and the team."

So now he has to work to stay there, Cousy and Auerbach say.

Work?

That's a fact of life for Kevin Gamble.

As Allen Pickering said, "He's a survivor."

Raveling after Gamble's junior season, and he was likewise impressed.

The Hawkeyes rode Gamble's game through the '87 NCAA tournament until he got into foul trouble against Nevada-Las Vegas. Without him on the floor, they lost.

Gamble, however, had drawn some attention. He was drafted in the third round that summer by Portland. And he did well in the Blazers' camp. "Playing with Clyde Drexler, Terry Porter and Kevin Duckworth every day in practice, I could see my ability. I knew I could play in the league," he recalled.

Rare as it is for a third round pick

to make a team, Gamble did. He lasted for nine games. "They made a trade for Richard Anderson, and I was the one to go," he told Jim Fenton. "I'll never forget it. We were in Philly at the time, and they came to my room to tell me I was cut. I was all excited that day because it was my chance to play against my idol, Doctor J, who was in his last year. It was tough because it was right before the game."

From there, he moved to the life of long bus rides in the CBA. He spent the rest of the 1987-88 season in Quad City. "I went down there with the attitude that I felt I was too good for that league, but once I got there

The jumper was just what Doc ordered.

Shaw opened up Boston's offense.

Shaw Time

The 1990-91 season had its share and ups and downs for Celtics' point guard Brian Shaw. Boston opened the season with a show of strength, and on the eve of the All-Star game, forward Kevin McHale said Shaw was the primary reason for the turnaround.

McHale even offered to give his place on the All-Star team to Shaw. The offer, of course, was no more than a gesture, but it's one that has been used in the past to acknowledge an overlooked teammate.

Impressing the Boston veterans hadn't been easy for Shaw. In essence, he had to replace long-time Celtics favorite Dennis Johnson.

"Dennis is the easiest guy I ever played with," Larry Bird said early last season. "He made things happen for me. Brian's a little different because he looks to penetrate, looks to make things happen for himself out there. But Brian's awful good. He does a little bit of everything. He rebounds, plays great defense. He's a total package."

From the start of the season, when he hit a game-winning basket in Chicago, Shaw established himself and steered Boston's running game.

"When he decided he was coming back, we had a meeting," coach Chris Ford said in December, "and a I told him that he was my point guard of the future, that I was gonna give him the ball and he was gonna run the show. He's done an outstanding job of being a distributor, of pushing that ball hard every time we get it.

"You can just see," Ford said of Shaw's influence on the team. "When we get the ball after a defensive stop, the ball finds its way to his hands, and the other four guys are on the fly. They want to beat each other down the floor to get a layup."

From the start of the season, when he hit a game-winning basket in Chicago, Shaw established himself and steered Boston's running game.

Getting established quickly meant that Shaw was able to provide leadership last season, something he hadn't been able to do as a rookie in 1988-89. "During my rookie year," he said, "it was like the wind was blowing, and I was going with the force of the wind. Now I feel like I'm making a little bit of a difference. When another team starts to make a run at us, I'm learning to step back and see what we have out there on the court and what we need to do, what adjustments we need to make."

Shaw's year playing with Il Messagero in Italy helped build this leadership quotient, Ford says. "The year he spent in Italy was developmental for him, even though he didn't play against NBA competition. He became the leader over there. He led the team in scoring and rebounding. The team was on his shoulders.

"Here the things we're asking him to do are very simple. Play good defense. Push the ball up the floor and get it to our scorers. He's done a very good job in those departments."

But Shaw's season hit a bump in early March when he severely sprained his right ankle against Portland. He missed three games, then probably came back too early. The ankle bothered him off and on throughout the rest of the season, making his troubles with shorter, quicker guards all the more troublesome.

Still, he managed to record 15 assists in a key win over Chicago March 31.

The playoffs, however, found the 6'6" Shaw on the down cycle in his game. His spotty play against Detroit led to a round of trade rumors after the season. The talk, though, seems to be mere rumor. The team's management apparently has no desire to give up on a young, promising player.

Veteran Celtics observers agree. "Point guards are scarce," said TV analyst Bob Cousy, who knows a thing or two about the position. "It wouldn't make sense to trade him."

Team president Red Auerbach said Shaw's struggles in the playoffs were understandable. After all, he only played a 30-game schedule last year in the Italian league and seemed to run out of gas as last season wore on.

"When you take a year off, it's hard to sustain a comeback over the long schedule," Auerbach said. "Plus he never really recovered completely from his sprained ankle.

"I think this year will be a better year for him. He'll come back strong."

An endorsement like that should bolster any young player's confidence. *Celtics Greenbook* caught up with Shaw at the close of last season and asked him the following questions about his progress.

Q: Have you found your comfort zone here in Boston?

A: Just about. I'm starting to feel really confident about myself and my game and assuming the leadership role when I'm on the court. I'm not really a rah-rah I'm not very vocal and emotional on the floor. That's something I'll have to gear myself towards.

Q: Because this team needs more rah-rah?

A: Right. Everyone here is pretty relaxed and laid-back. Reggie Lewis is quiet and shy. So is Kevin Gamble. Bird, too. Everybody goes out and plays hard, but they're quiet.

Q: Is there emotion underneath all of that quiet?

A: I think so. I think they all have their fire inside of them.

Q: What developments did you see in your game this past season?

A: Just overall confidence. I don't do anything spectacular, or out of the ordinary. I just do a lot of the little things. I like to get the ball to guys in the right spot. I like to pick it up defensively to get us running. I try to do a lot of intangibles. You can't pick up the paper and judge what I do by looking at the stats.

Q: As you become more of a pro point guard, are assists more important to you? Is that the first item you look at on the stat sheets?

A: Yeah it is. I look at that and the number of shots that each player on the floor got. You try to have balance and to have everybody around the 10- or 11-shot range, at least. When Reggie is hot, I try to look for him a little more. The same with Bird when he's in there and feeling it.

Q: Do you have specific goals set for statistics and for matching up with the top point guards in the league?

Shaw is beginning to find himself as a pro point guard.

A: I try to reach the double-figure mark in scoring. Ideally I would like to be around a triple double, whether its 10-10-10 or what. If I could, that's what I'd shoot for night in and night out.

Defensively, I would not want the other team to get anything easy. I try to bother the other point guards and be a little physical with them. When they get it inside to the big men, I try to come down and reach for the ball,

just let 'em know I'm there so they can feel my presence. That makes 'em work for everything they get.

Q: Who are the toughest matchups for you around the league?

A: Because I'm one of the taller point guards, I don't particularly like playing teams that set a lot of screens, especially for the shorter, quicker point guards like Kevin Johnson or Tim Hardaway or John Stockton. It's already difficult enough

Shaw's a scrapper.

to try to stop these guys, because they're great ballhandlers and they're very quick and low to the ground. But then you have some big guys setting screens to help free 'em up, and it's all the more difficult.

I'm more effective when I'm playing someone my size, or maybe even a little bit bigger. I think I have pretty fair quickness for my size. In the Eastern Conference, most of the point guards are medium-sized. I have an advantage against them because I can go to the low post and get easy buckets.

Q: Magic Johnson, of course, is a big man playing the post. Have you studied him much?

A: Yeah. Growing up on the West Coast, I've watched him for years and years. He's big and strong. You just have to try and establish yourself

> **I'm more effective when I'm playing someone my size, or maybe even a little bit bigger. I think I have pretty fair quickness for my size.**
> **—Brian Shaw**

against him early on. If you let him back you down and have his way at the beginning of the game, then the refs are gonna call fouls his way as you go along. If you go out there and show him you're not gonna let him push you around, then you can play pretty physical.

Q: Is it one of your goals to add some size and strength up top? Do

you want to be a post-up point guard like Magic?

A: I do. Ideally I'd like to weigh maybe 10 pounds more. But my metabolism isn't going to allow that right now. I eat a lot, but I'm just so active it's tough for me to put on weight.

Q: After playing in Italy was it difficult to return to Boston?

A: Not at all. People don't understand my situation. I was ready for whatever was gonna take place. Actually it was a lot smoother than I anticipated. I've gotten some crazy fan mail, where people have been very upset and said, "How could you do something like this to our team?" But there hasn't been anything real serious. Most people have been nice.

Pump It Up

He's gonna be good. You can sense it. Which means his name and charisma are bound to generate a lot of headlines over the years to come. Just imagine the word-play.

Let's see, there's Dee-lightful and Dee-lighted, and "He's a Dee-light."

He'll play Dee-fense with Dee-termination. Victories will be Dee-cisive. Opponents will be Dee-feated and Dee-stroyed and Dee-molished and Dee-nied and Dee-pressed. When he blocks shots, they'll be Dee-jected or Dee-ferred. When he steals the ball, opponents will be Dee-prived. When the game is on the line, he'll Dee-liver.

Plus there'll be a whole new section in the dictionary of Boston Hoops Jargon. It will include:

Dee-bonair. Reebok's new ad slogan to infuriate the opposition.

Dee-face. A job. When he hits that jumper. In yo' face.

Dee-feat. A special Deedunk.

Here Come Dee Judge. His new poster issued before the 1992 Gatorade Slam Dunk competition.

Dee-frost. His super good Dee-fense. Like chill out.

Dee-cember. When he has a great month right before Xmas.

Dee-lirium. When the Garden gets loud over a Deedunk.

Dee-range. The distance on his jumper.

Dee-mon. How he's described by his fans in Jamaica.

Dee-scribes. Writers who write about Dee-mon.

Dee-fine. The money he'll pay to the Commissioner after a brouhaha.

Dee-duce. His two-pointer. Not a trey.

Dee-votees. Fans who cast his name on All-Star ballots.

Homey On Dee Range. The rap song written about Dee-mon's exploits.

Brown tied the year up in a nice bow by raising his level of play in the playoffs and showing that he could be counted on when the pressure hit the high side.

This may seem a bit excessive for somebody whose real name is DeCovan Kadell Brown. But it appears that after a mere 12 months on the job he has qualified as Boston's newest and youngest legend.

Brown himself admits as much. "I'm a Celtic through and through," he says.

After all, he had quite a storybook season last year. Coming off the Celtics' bench, he played well and shot well as an NBA freshman, averaging 8.7 points over 82 games. He showed a tough defensive nose and an ability to push the ball on offense. Beyond that he won the Slam Dunk Tournament during All-Star Weekend, then he tied the year up in a nice bow by raising his level of play in the playoffs and showing that he could be counted on when the pressure hit the high side. He averaged 12.2 points, 4 rebounds and 3.8 assists and shot .491 from the floor during the playoffs.

Against Detroit, he put on quite a Dee-mon-stration, averaging 15.5 points and 31.8 minutes per game. He scored 15 points in the fourth quarter of Game 2 of that series on his way to a 22-point night. And the next game, he had nine rebounds to go with his 13 points and six assists.

With all of that, you might expect the Celtics' braintrust would be trumpeting their "find" with the 19th pick of the first round of the 1990 draft. But Red Auerbach and company are not striking up any brass bands. Instead, they're playing a cautious note of optimism heading into the 1991-92 season. Mainly they hoping Brown doesn't hit a sophomore slump.

"He had a fabulous year," Auerbach said. "But the big test is this year when they start zeroing in on him. A rookie very often comes out with a good year, then he thinks he's got it made and doesn't work enough. They start zeroing in on him, and he falls back. I don't think that's going to happen with this kid because he's focused pretty good. But often that does happen."

Such caution should help knock down the media expectations. But there's little need to worry about Dee-termined's work ethic. He didn't have to, but he arrived in Boston's 1991 rookie camp just to get in the extra work.

The issue, though, is not just how Brown plays, but where he plays. Celtics' TV analyst Bob Cousy expressed concern that the team

"Dee Brown has done everything that I had hoped he could do," Ford says.

might plan to make Dee the starting point guard before he's ready. "It would be a mistake to turn the reins over to him this year," Cousy said.

Auerbach agreed with that assessment: "He's not ready yet. He needs more experience than he's had."

Regardless of the experience, Cousy still isn't convinced that Brown's a point guard. He seems more of a shooting guard. And he may not be a guard at all. After all, he played a good amount of small forward at Jacksonville University.

Whatever the position, Cousy says there's little question that Dee Brown is a player. "He's one of these Frank Ramsey types," the Celtics' point guard emeritus explained. "You put him in the game, and he's gonna do something."

For example, just watch him play Dee-fense, Cousy says. "His nose is almost on the floor when he's guarding the ball."

That enthusiasm is shared by coach Chris Ford. "Dee Brown has done everything that I had hoped he could do," Ford says. "He plays good defense. He can push the ball offensively. He presents good combinations. I can play him alongside Brian Shaw. It's a luxury having the ball in either one's hands on the break.

"The thing a lot of people didn't realize is how well Dee can shoot the ball. There were a lot of questions as to whether he could knock down that outside shot. From what we saw on film, we liked his shooting ability.

"Although he couldn't play at rookie camp because he hadn't signed his contract, he came in and shot some. He showed us he had the confidence in his shot, and that gave me some early confidence to play him."

As might be expected, all of this

Dee-termined to score.

has been immensely pleasing to Brown. "It feels good that I could blend in," he says. "You hear the stories, rookies don't do this; rookies don't play.

"Boston has been known for guards who could knock down the 15-to 20-footers. Dennis Johnson would hit those shots and break hearts.

"I put upon myself last summer the job of shooting jumpers. I knew that in the NBA I was gonna have to spot up and hit that open shot. Then I got drafted by Boston, and I knew that open shot was even more important. I knew my job was not to be the first option on offense, or the second option, or even the third or fourth option. My job was to be ready when

my came around."

It seems that the 6'1" Brown's option has come around much quicker than he or anyone else expected. His 42-inch vertical leap has added an interesting new twist to Celtics' Mystique. That became obvious with his Slam Dunk victory, which stirred a lot of old Celtics' Pride.

"It's something different in Boston," Brown said at the time. "There's never been a Celtic in the slam dunk contest. Everybody was excited."

It even brought old Celtics out of the woodwork as Dee practiced his stuff in the days leading up to All-Star Weekend in Charlotte. John Havlicek appeared at one Celtic practice at

He's been solid off the bench.

Hellenic College in Brookline and sprung his ideas on Brown. He suggested that Dee lie on his back, then suddenly spring up, catch a thrown ball and dunk it.

"You're surprised when you get all this advice from guys who can't dunk," Brown said, laughing. "Havlicek gave me a lot of advice. He was talking to me about what the crowd likes, what the judges like. I don't know how he knows this stuff, but I listened to him."

Equipment Manager Joe Qatato also had some creative dunk ideas, and suggested that Brown deal him a cut of the winnings.

Brian Shaw, Reggie Lewis and Joe Kleine all offered suggestions, too.

Joe Kleine?

"You can't really win a dunk contest by yourself," Brown said. "You have to have ideas from other people."

But when show time arrived, it all came down to Dee. He immediately drew the attention of the crowd and judges by pausing before each effort to pump his Pumps seven times. Afterward, Brown Dee-nied that he was pumping the shoes to boost his shoe contract and marketability.

"It's a show really, and that's all I was thinking about," he said. "The pump is just something that I wanted to do."

His repétoire of slams included a

Brown's a leaper.

no-peek jam, with his face buried in the crook of his arm.

"Being a little guy, I threw a couple of 'em down pretty hard," he said afterward. "That was one thing I wanted to stress, that I could throw 'em down hard. I was so pumped up, that a couple of things I did, I was surprised.

"But, at my size, you have to be different."

That doesn't seem as if it'll be a problem for Dee-lightful. He's refreshingly unpretentious. At All-Star Weekend, he was an unabashed star gazer at the opening media reception.

"I'm still a fan," he explained. "It was great shaking Kevin Johnson's hand and being around Magic and Michael."

Brown, of course, has very quickly found an identity among his charismatic elders. In fact, even before All-Star weekend, Reebok was working on his special shoe, a lighter version of the Pump.

"What do you call it?" one writer asked. "Dee Pump?"

Brown laughs easily at such fun. Why shouldn't he? After all, he's Dee-lightful.

Lewis has found a home in the Garden.

The steady shot.

Right On, Reggie

Considering that he won't turn 26 until November 1991, it's hard to think of Reggie Lewis as a wise old Celtics veteran. But outside of the Big Three — Robert Parish, Larry Bird and Kevin McHale—no one on the team has spent more time on the parquet. Over the past four years, Reggie has quietly established himself as the team's next generation of leadership.

And he likes filling the role.

"Besides the three veterans and myself, everybody else is practically new," Lewis says. "It's a whole different atmosphere around here. Everybody else is newer or younger."

He is heading into his fifth pro season in Boston, and at a time when most young pro players are just coming into their own, the 6'7" Lewis has already arrived.

"He's a worker," said team president Red Auerbach. "He just keeps getting better. And his scoring isn't padded with late-game statistics. He hits the shots when we need 'em."

"The verdict is unanimous," agreed TBS analyst Rick

Community-minded.

51

Looking for the open man.

Barry in his scouting report. "Lewis will be a big-time scorer for a long time to come."

Reggie has drawn such praise by showing marked and consistent improvement in each of his four seasons. The 1991-92 campaign was no exception. He set career highs in several regular-season categories, including:

• Boosting his scoring average to 18.7 points per game;
• Setting a single-game high in scoring of 42 points (against New York in April);
• Blocking 85 shots;
• Upping his free-throw accuracy to .826;
• Averaging 5.2 rebounds per game, among the best for NBA guards.

As a result of all this, coach Chris Ford simply couldn't afford to have Lewis on the bench. He played 2,878 minutes over 79 games, 36.4 minutes per game, another career high.

But the real evidence of Lewis' maturity came in the playoffs, where for the third straight year he led the team in scoring. Each of the past three seasons, he has upped his performance to meet the Celtics' challengers. In the 11 games of 1991, he averaged 22.4 points, another career high. Plus he averaged better than six rebounds per game.

"With a multitude of weapons, Lewis is the prototypical scorer," Barry says. "Underlying it all is his athleticism. A wiry 6'7", he plays bigger because he can jump out of the gym. He also runs the floor exceptionally well and is extremely quick. He has a superb first step and can beat you off the dribble, then either jam it or make one of those patented runners in the lane."

Never known to use such compliments freely, Barry also marveled at Lewis' defensive development over the past four seasons. "He has a lot going for him defensively," Barry said. "He's quick, has long arms, moves his feet well and can jump. Other two guards going against Lewis have a tough time because of his size."

For Lewis, the first four years in Boston have been trying but rewarding. Injuries to Larry Bird have interrupted the team's high level of success, but they also allowed Lewis to get the playing time he needed to establish his game during the 1988-89 season. He said he hated for his opportunity to come at Bird's expense, but it also made him more determined to make the best of his playing time.

Now, he is firmly established as one of the team's offensive leaders, a role he relishes despite the added responsibility.

"The biggest thing is the pressure the fans put on you. And the media," he said. "Playing in Boston, they have such big expectations of you. You have to go out and produce every night."

That, of course, seems to be no problem for him. Although he was wracked by back pain last winter, he turned in some of his best performances in January and March, recording 12 rebounds each against New York, Washington and Utah, which tied his career high.

It seems that Lewis is no where near peaking yet. Year after year, he continues to improve. Unlike many young players in the league today, he isn't trafficking on his potential—he's realizing it.

As Rick Barry says, "Reggie has arrived."

In traffic.

Reggie shows Mychal Thompson his good stuff.

Cowens was the league MVP and Heinsohn the coach of the year in 1973.

The Sensational '70s

Editor's note: Celtics' center Dave Cowens was elected to the Naismith Memorial Basketball Hall of Fame in February 1991, along with former Boston guard Nate "Tiny" Archibald, bringing to 21 the number of former Celtics elected to the Hall. What follows is a retrospective of Cowens' glory years with Boston, 1974 and 1976, when he led the team to NBA titles.

After leading the Celtics to 11 NBA championships over his 13-year career, center Bill Russell retired in 1969, and Boston's winning ways came to a halt. The Celtics finished next to last in the Eastern Division with a 34-48 record in 1970.

But the team swiftly pushed its way back to the top of the NBA power structure over the next two seasons. For opponents around the league, it wasn't a welcome sight. There was Red Auerbach again with that damn cigar.

Red rebuilt his Celtics much the same way he had constructed the team's original dynasty. He went for the unorthodox. And he found most of what he wanted right in the college draft. When he couldn't get it there, Auerbach fell back on the old standby—he outfoxed his opponents in a trade.

The Celtics drafted Don "Duck" Chaney out of the University of Houston in 1968. The next year they got JoJo White from the University of Kansas. Both players would require a little seasoning, but before long the pair would make a splendid backcourt.

Red's real coup, though, was the center.

As the story goes, Auerbach saw

Red rebuilt his Celtics much the same way he had constructed the team's original dynasty. He went for the unorthodox.

Dave Cowens play only one college game. The more the Celtics' general manager watched the Florida State center, the more he liked him. Cowens played so well that Auerbach began hoping he would mess up. There were other pro scouts at the game, and Auerbach didn't want them to get too excited about what they saw. Finally, after about five minutes, Auerbach got up and left the game. On the way out, he tried to act disgusted. He was hoping the other scouts would think Cowens didn't have it.

As things worked out, Auerbach got just the guy he wanted. The Celtics picked fourth in the 1970 draft. Detroit took Bob Lanier of St. Bonaventure with the first pick. The

San Diego Rockets selected Rudy Tomjanovich second, and the Atlanta Hawks went with Pete Maravich third.

Boston took Cowens fourth, only the Celtics' G.M. still wasn't sure what to do with him. He figured that at 6'8" Cowens was too short to be an NBA center. But in training camp later that summer, Cowens resisted being moved to forward.

"I wanted to play center," Cowens recalled. "That's what I had always played. But they were the experts, you know."

Auerbach struggled with the problem, then decided to phone Bill Russell for a bit of advice.

Let him play where he wants, Russell told Auerbach. "No one's going to intimidate that kid."

It didn't take Auerbach long to see what Russell was talking about. Playing against Wilt Chamberlain, Cowens scored 33 points and had 22 rebounds in an exhibition game.

That and his performance in several summer league games convinced the Celtic brass that he could be a center. Given the chance, Cowens played the position the way no one ever had before. He was too small to bang around in the low post with his larger opponents. So he used his other assets. He was a fine leaper and he had great speed and long arms. More importantly, he showed the aggressiveness of a linebacker.

"I don't worry about injuries," he said cockily. "I'm the one going a little bit nutty out there. I don't get hit because I'm the one doing the hitting."

His speed and agility allowed him to play corner-to-corner. It also meant that the Celtics had the best switching defense in the league, because Cowens could switch to a smaller man and not lose a step.

"He adds a different dimension to Boston's game," Chicago's Norm Van Lier said not long after Cowens came into the league. "He has a great defensive range on a horizontal rather than a vertical plane. He'll meet me at the top of the key, spread those long arms and make it almost impossible to pass off."

Over time, Cowens proved he could neutralize the giants of his era—Abdul-Jabbar, Chamberlain, Lanier and Thurmond—with his quickness. "He's so quick he's like a 6'9" Jerry West," said Jerry Lucas of the Knicks. "One minute he's standing in front of you and the next he's gone, rolling in toward the basket or straight up in the air shooting his jumper. It's like he disappears."

"He's the toughest I've ever played against," Thurmond allowed.

Off the court, Cowens was a man of the times. His behavior showed a heavy streak of zaniness. The early 1970s had a '60s flavor to it. People looked for the new and different. "It wasn't a time to be too conventional," he recalled with a smile.

He invested in a catfish farm in British Honduras, and during his second season in Boston he became so involved in an auto mechanics course that Auerbach asked him to drop it. He was given to wearing beat-up courdoroy trousers and plaid shirts, and his musical tastes ran from bluegrass to Beethoven. "I got bored sitting around," Cowens explained. "So I started doing a lot of different things. To me, that was the smart thing to do. It kept me out of trouble."

Even for a red-head, he was high strung. By game time each night he was a ball of nervous energy, ready to explode with the opening jump. He would dash here and there with reckless abandon, diving for loose balls, giving hard fouls, shooting his nifty left-handed hook, and rebounding like a fool. He celebrated good plays by head-butting his teammates. "Dave's got one hard head," Don Nelson told the writers. That was true in more ways than one.

As a young pro, Cowens was hesitant to shoot from outside, until his teammates finally convinced him

Cowens was unorthodox, but effective.

that the team needed it. With a little work, he added a shot with some decent range to it, although he never did work hard enough to develop his right hand. Still, his game was enough to take the Celtics where they needed to go.

Tommy Heinsohn, the erstwhile gunner, had followed Russell as the Celtics' coach. Heinsohn's goal was to make them a running team again, and Cowens was perfect for it. Heinsohn figured Cowens was faster in the 100-yard dash than any player in the league.

But Cowens couldn't solve all of Heinsohn's problems. He faced the task of getting the old Celtics to accept the new batch of youngsters. Eventually the Boston newcomers would mix well with the holdovers from the Russell years—John Havlicek, Nelson and Satch Sanders.

But it wasn't automatic. Heinsohn's major developmental work involved the guards. White was a gazelle, but it took him a while to become accustomed to Heinsohn's running game. Thinking of the future, Heinsohn decided to bench starting guards Em Bryant and Larry Siegfried during the 1969-70 season and replace them with Chaney and White, then a rookie. It wasn't a popular move in Boston at the time, but the younger guards had the speed and skills to run. Heinsohn knew he had to get them the necessary experience. The move would become even less popular when Heinsohn gave up Siegfried, Havlicek's good friend and teammate from Ohio State, in the expansion draft that spring. But the Celtics had just been through a 34-48 season, and the coach knew he had to do something.

White learned to run the offense.

Yet even with playing time White presented a particular problem for Heinsohn. He had immense talent and the confidence to go with it. But he had played in a controlled, walk-it-up offense at Kansas and had little experience with the running game, particularly the version Heinsohn wanted to run, which was based on the philosophy of overloading players to one side. It required complicated decision-making and good experience running the break.

Because he was so talented and proud, White at first rejected Heinsohn's attempts to teach him the intricacies of playing the point in the Celtics' offense. Heinsohn backed off and tried another direction. Instead of overwhelming White with dramatic change, Heinsohn worked in the new approach a bit at a time. Eventually, player and coach came to an understanding, and when they did, the team ran off at a new level.

The 6'5" Chaney was the other backcourt ingredient, a superb defender. He had been a high-school All-America at McKinley High in Baton Rouge, Louisiana, before going to Houston to play for Guy Lewis. There he performed in the shadow of Elvin Hayes but was a critical element to the Cougars' pressing defense. "Chaney had long arms and great anticipation for a pass," Lewis said. "We didn't keep steals in those days, and there's no telling how many he

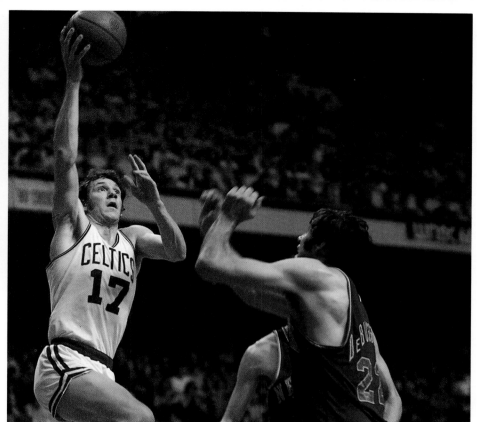

Havlicek was the veteran.

Chaney was a fine defensive guard. (Photos by Ron Koch)

had. But it would have been some kind of record."

He started at guard for his junior and senior years, and averaged double-figure scoring both seasons, although most of his points came as layups, off steals and and turnovers. He didn't have an outside shot, but he had all the mental skills to be a great defensive guard. "Chaney was a super leader, a quiet leader but a super one all the same," Lewis said. "He knew the game of basketball in and out."

At first, that didn't appear to be enough to allow him to make it in the NBA. He played little his first season and shot just .319 from the floor. But Heinsohn made Chaney one of his pet projects, and the two spent hours working on Chaney's shot. After a time, Chaney became a pretty decent shooter, adding yet another block to Boston's rebuilding job.

This new edition of the Celtics wasn't real pretty, but it was a winner. They nailed down 44 games in 1971 and 56 in 1972, making their progress obvious. Still, the team's veterans, particularly Havlicek, were frustrated by the imprecision of this younger group. Havlicek had been used to the crisp ballhandling and overall dominance of the Celtics teams featuring Cousy and K.C. Jones and Russell, and with each transitional season his patience seemed a little thinner.

Fortunately, the player arrived before the 1972-73 season that cemented their chemistry. Auerbach knew he needed a power forward, someone to help Cowens with the rebounding. The Boston boss finally was able to obtain Paul Silas from Phoenix for the NBA rights to Charlie Scott, who was playing in the ABA and about to jump to the senior league.

An eight-year pro, Silas had always been on the chunky side. But the season before coming to the Celtics he had trimmed to a svelte 6'7" 230-pounder and was ready to join Heinsohn's version of the Boston marathon. He came in and played like a charm, albeit a bullish one that first season. Silas pulled down 1,039

Cowens had great mobility for a center.

rebounds (13 per game), while Cowens got 1329, making Boston the best board team in the league. It was the first time in league history that two teammates had each gotten 1,000 rebounds.

All that defensive rebounding, of course, was just what the doctor ordered for Heinsohn's running game. The Celtics ran off to a 68-14 record, the best in the club's distinguished history. They were a terror to face. But then an unprecedented thing happened in Boston. The two best teams in basketball, the Celtics and the Knicks, met in the Eastern Conference finals, and in the decisive seventh game, in Boston Garden no less, the Celtics stumbled. They lost and watched New York go on to trample Los Angeles for the world championship.

It was a bitter, bitter ending to a bright beginning.

REGARDING KAREEM

As Boston fans hoped, the Celtics opened the 1973-74 season with a vengeance, racing out to a 30-7 start. From there, though, they grew strangely complacent and barely played .500 ball over the remainder of

the schedule.

Fortunately, they had the luck of the Irish with them. The Eastern Conference was a bit weak with the Knicks aging and injured. Boston finished 56-26, good enough for the best record in the conference, but short of Milwaukee's 59-33 mark in the Western. The Buffalo Braves with Robert McAdoo created problems for Boston in the first round of the playoffs, but Havlicek played well enough to help them advance, 4-2. The Knicks, with Willis Reed and Dave DeBusschere injured, fell rather easily, 4-1, and Boston advanced to the Finals for the first time ever without Bill Russell.

Milwaukee had held serve in the Western, dropping Los Angeles 4-1, then Chicago 4-0 in the conference finals. The outcomes provided something of a prize for pure basketball fans because the two best teams in the pro game were meeting in the championship round. Their matchup was an invigorating clash of styles. With Kareem Abdul-Jabbar and his famed sky hook, the Bucks were the consummate half-court team and nearly unstoppable when the big center got the ball in the post. For this to happen, Bucks coach Larry

Costello and his assistant, Hubie Brown, had devised myriad schemes, all encased in Milwaukee's massive playbook which detailed options upon options.

On the other hand, the Celtics were a small, quick, pressing and running team that approached things from basic simplicity. Their starting front line ran 6'7", 6'8" and 6'5". Heinsohn knew if his troops were going to win, the press would have to do it for them. They'd have to take the ball away before the Bucks ever got it upcourt to the big guy.

This, of course, highlighted the crucial glitch for the Bucks. Lucius Allen, who shared the ballhandling chores with Oscar Robertson, had torn up his knee slipping on a warmup jersey at the close of the season and was lost for the playoffs. Robertson was 35 and in the last season of his career. He faced the vaunted Boston press virtually alone. The Bucks had Bobby Dandridge at forward and Jon McGlocklin and off guard, but their test would be to get the ball up the floor against Chaney.

The basketball purists also relished the idea of the small, quick Cowens meeting the giant, athletic Abdul-Jabbar in the Finals. Under the Celtics' scheme, they would leave their center to fend for himself man-to-man. Fear, it seemed, was a good motivator for the redhead. As a rookie, Cowens had watched helplessly as Kareem scored 53 against him. He knew it could happen any time. "No one wants to look used and foolish out on the court," Cowens told the writers covering the Finals. "Our style doesn't give me much help because the other guys are off pressing, so I have to try and stop him by myself and remember that if he has a big game I won't be the first guy it's happened to. But I have a couple of things going for me. When the guys are off pressing, they're really helping me. The better they press, the less often Kareem's going to get the ball. And on offense I can score from the outside, which puts him at a disadvantage."

That, in short, became a blueprint for the series, the basis on which

Don Nelson came off the bench.

each team made its adjustments. It quickly developed into one of the most engrossing championship rounds in league history, one in which the home-court advantage meant almost nothing.

The Celtics wasted little time in playing their hand. In the first quarter of Game 1 in Milwaukee, they harassed Robertson and Allen's replacement, Ron "Fritz" Williams, into numerous turnovers and ran to a 35-19 lead. The Bucks never solved their ballhandling problems and watched the Celtics dance off to a 98-83 shocker. Kareem had scored 35, but the offense remained in disarray.

"If we could just get the damn ball out of the backcourt, our problems would be solved," Costello lamented.

The Bucks coach shifted strategy a bit for Game 2, pushing all the help upcourt and leaving Robertson to face Chaney alone. The new plan

meant that Milwaukee conceded 22 turnovers, but it worked. Kareem scored 36 points, but more importantly, the big center was able to set up and run the Bucks' offense in the halfcourt. He set picks, and he passed, which was a factor in Dandridge scoring 24. On the defensive end, Kareem forced Cowens into shooting 3 of 13. When the game came down to a final shot and Cowens was open for a running hook in the lane, Abdul-Jabbar swooped down and blocked it. From there, the Bucks took it in overtime, 105-96, to even the series at 1-1 as it headed to Boston.

Cowens responded in Game 3 with a determination to concentrate on his outside shot. Despite foul trouble that reduced him to 32 minutes of playing time, he scored 30 (7 of 10 shooting from the field in the first half). The Celtics press also stepped up the pressure, forcing 11 first-quarter turnovers and helping them to a 21-point lead. With Cowens in foul trouble, Henry Finkel, Boston's little used 7-footer, did an admirable job of spot defense on Kareem, who finished with 26.

At game's end, the Bucks had turned the ball over 27 times, enough for a 95-83 Boston win.

Costello knew his team was in real trouble. McGlocklin had sprained an ankle early on and was unable to help. The Boston press had taken Williams' confidence. The Bucks needed somebody to step forward at guard. So Costello pulled in 6'7" Mickey Davis, a substitute forward who had played little guard over his three-year career. Davis, though, was tall enough to present major problems for White. When Davis began scoring in Game 4, Heinsohn was forced to shift the taller Chaney to cover him, thus cutting the heart out of Boston's press. Robertson brought the ball upcourt relatively unmolested. Davis scored 15, while Kareem got the ball in the halfcourt, where he shredded the Celtics for 34 points and six assists. Milwaukee got the lead and kept it down the stretch for a 97-89 win. That quickly, the fortunes seemed to have reversed themselves. The Bucks headed back to Milwaukee with the homecourt advantage and a series reduced to three games. Good as it looked at the time, the homecourt advantage proved worthless.

The Bucks had concentrated most of their defensive efforts on stopping 34-year-old John Havlicek, the silent but deadly part of Boston's operation.

"When things are swinging easy, we all get in the flow of it," Paul Silas told the writers. "And sometimes then it almost looks like we ignore John. But when things don't go well, we look to him all the time to make the tough play. We probably do it too much. Sometimes I'll have an open shot and still pass to him even though he's farther out and two guys are on him. We do this instinctively because he has usually been the guy who's turned bad moments into good ones for us."

White drives against Oscar. (Koch photo)

Havlicek stepped through the double teams to the forefront over the balance of the series. An incredibly conditioned athlete, he was able to keep running on offense and moving and crouching on defense when players with half his experience were winded. It was a natural gift, Havlicek often explained, and he used it to the fullest. He and the Celtics wore down the Bucks with their motion in Game 5, regaining the series edge, 3-2, with a 96-77 win that set up a classic Game 6 back in Boston.

The situation offered the fans Kareem at his best, although that wasn't exactly what the packed house at the Garden had in mind on May 10. Cowens found foul trouble early and watched from the bench as Milwaukee took a 12-point lead in the first half. The Celtics were down six late in the game, but they came back to force overtime. With a little over a

Cowens scores in Milwaukee.

Kareem hits the big shot.

minute left, Havlicek hit a long jumper to tie it at 86, then Robertson was caught in a 24-second violation as regulation expired. In the first extra period, Milwaukee led 90-88 when Chaney got a steal and zipped the ball to Havlicek. Kareem was back on defense and forced him to take a pull-up jumper. Havlicek missed but got the long rebound and scored to send the game to a second overtime.

There Havlicek scored nine of Boston's 11 points. He had the ball on the right baseline at 0:07, and the Boston bench screamed for a timeout. Instead, Havlicek lofted a rainbow over Kareem's outstretched hand. Good, for a 101-100 lead. It looked like champagne time.

But the Bucks got a timeout, where for some strange reason they figured Kareem shouldn't take the shot. Instead, he was to set a pick for McGlocklin, who had been hampered by the sprained ankle. When McGlocklin couldn't get free, Abdul-Jabbar moved to the right of the lane. He looked for the open man, but Boston had all the options covered. So he dribbled to the baseline, turned and put up the skyhook from 17 feet. Swish. 102-101, Milwaukee.

"That was a hell of a shot," Cowens recalled nearly two decades later. "I haven't seen too many people hit a pressure shot from that far out."

The Celtics got a final desperation heave, but that was it. Kareem had made a shot that left him lying awake in bed night, tingling with excitement. He wasn't the only one. Rick Barry, who worked the game as a television analyst, thought it just might have been the best game ever played.

The series was tied at three and going back to Milwaukee. The circumstances called for special efforts, so on the eve of the game, Auerbach called together the entire Boston brain trust, Cousy included. They decided that for this final game, they would abandon their single-man coverage of Kareem and go for the double- and triple-teams.

"The meeting has gotten a lot of attention over the years," Cowens said. "But it wasn't that big a deal. We were just going to throw a little

different look at 'em defensively."

With less defensive load, Cowens turned his thoughts to offense. He had shot a miserable 5 of 16 from the floor in Game 6. He remedied that in the first half of the seventh game, making 8 of 13 as Boston loped out to a lead and jogged down the stretch for a 102-87 win and another Boston title.

Cowens finished with 28 points, 14 rebounds and an incalcuable defensive effort on Abdul-Jabbar. It had been Cowens' first championship series of any sort. "It was pretty exciting for me," he said. "It was fairly nerve wracking."

Havlicek had scored 16 while continuing to draw the Bucks' defensive attention. Soaked in pink champagne, he grinned broadly in the

> **Cowens finished with 28 points, 14 rebounds and an incalcuable defensive effort on Abjul-Jabbar. It had been Cowens' first championship series of any sort. "It was pretty exciting for me," he said. "It was fairly nerve wracking."**

Celtics' lockerroom afterward and accepted the MVP award. This young team had finally lived up to his standards and Bill Russell's tradition. Back in Boston, they were shifting things around in the Garden rafters to make room for title banner number twelve.

SETTING THE SUNS

The 1975-76 NBA season had a symmetry to it, and that symmetry involved a trade. The Phoenix Suns and the Celtics traded guards and then met in the Finals to see who got the better of the deal. In that regard, the deal brought to mind the 1956 trade between the St. Louis Hawks and Boston. Auerbach had traded center Ed Macauley and forward Cliff

Hagan for the draft pick that would become Bill Russell. That deal worked pretty well for both teams. They met in the Finals four of the next five years.

The 1976 deal didn't hurt the Suns either. It allowed them to move from a lower-rung club right to the championship bracket. Phoenix had traded Charlie Scott to the Celtics for sharpshooter Paul Westphal, and a phenomenal season followed.

The Suns, an eight-year-old franchise, finished the 1975-76 regular schedule at 42-40, but had gotten better with each game, and by the playoffs were the best in the Western Conference.

First Phoenix tripped Seattle and followed that by upsetting Golden State in a seven-game showdown. The Suns tooks the seventh game in Oakland, 94-86, by holding Rick Barry scoreless for nearly 30 minutes.

The Celtics filled in the other side of the bracket, although they weren't the same team that had won in 1974. Seeking more money, Don Chaney had moved on to the American Basketball Association. And Westphal, the third guard, had gone to the Suns. Scott, a slight but wonderfully gifted guard at 6'5", 175 pounds, joined JoJo White in the Boston backcourt, which led to immediate speculation that one basketball wouldn't be enough for the two of them. That did prove to be a consideration but not a problem. Boston adjusted and finished atop the Eastern Conference regular-season standings with a 54-28 record. Then in the playoffs, they brushed aside Buffalo and Cleveland in a pair of six-game series.

Coached by Heinsohn, the Celtics still played that tough old brand of ball. In a development never equalled before or since, Havlicek, Cowens and Silas—the starting frontcourt—were named to the league's all-defensive first-team. That and their tradition made them big favorites against the Suns. There was even talk of a sweep.

After all, Phoenix was a young team with a young coach, John MacLeod, who had a reputation as a

Backup center Henry Finkel (29) guards Kareem in the '74 Finals.

The Suns do a takedown of Silas in Phoenix.

Charlie Scott shoots over the Phoenix defense.

Nellie and Hondo beneath Adams' reach.

Havlicek boxes out. (Koch photos)

motivator. He did it with his looks as well as his words. His looks ran to stylish array of vested suits that projected an upscale sophistication. His tastes ran from plaids to pinstripes, or just about anything that suggested class.

But he was much more than just another guy sporting a necktie. MacLeod had solid ideas about tough defense and team offense. Best of all, his youth was peppered by his idealism. The whole package spelled enthusiasm.

"MacLeod would have made a fanatastic preacher," Westphal said of his coach. "He sees a crippled guy and he comes in and uses it in his pre-game talk."

Heinsohn, on the other hand, had once used 72 "bleeps" during his halftime talk for a Christmas Day game, Westphal said. How did he know? "I sat in the back of the lockerroom and counted them," he explained.

All of MacLeod's goodness didn't count for much at the start of the season. His Suns were picked to finish last. After all, they started two rookies, Alvan Adams at center and Ricky Sobers at guard, and two well-traveled veterans at forward, Garfield Heard and Curtis Perry.

Whatever Phoenix hoped to accomplish, Westphal was the designated driver. A fourth-year player out of Southern Cal, he was 6'4" and a whiz at moving without the ball. That made him all the more important to Phoenix because he could get his shots without a lot of help. He also possessed acrobatic moves that thrilled the fans. A backup at Boston, he became better with each game he started in Phoenix. Over the last half of season, his average soared to better than 23 points per game. Plus, he wasn't a bad defensive player and showed a knack for slipping into the passing lanes unnoticed to snatch the ball.

Sobers, out of Nevada-Las Vegas, hadn't been billed as a big-time player but joined Westphal in the backcourt when veteran Dick Van Arsdale, 33, fractured his left arm (he returned by the playoffs). Sobers was

Westphal was traded to Phoenix for Charlie Scott.

a surprisingly good ballhandler for a rookie and showed a fiesty streak that allowed him to play older than his years.

Adams was nearly as unsung as Sobers, although he wound up winning the rookie-of-the-year award by averaging 19 points and nine rebounds as the Suns' starting center. He had planned to be a doctor but gave up his senior year at Oklahoma to collect an NBA salary. The young center had matured over the season with the rest of the team, Westphal said. "Before he'd explode for big scoring games, but now he's more consistent. He's the backbone of the team. We wouldn't be anywhere near the playoffs without him."

When MacLeod needed more

experience in the game he went to former Laker Keith Erickson off the bench. The Suns also got decent minutes out of 6'10" Dennis Awtrey in the frontcourt and mid-sized Nate Hawthorne. Once healthy, Van Arsdale helped in the backcourt. All told, they played with a conviction that impressed all their opponents.

"Phoenix is ambitious, hungry and has great energy," said Phil Smith of the Warriors after the Western finals.

Age, as usual, was the dominant theme with the Celtics. Havlicek had torn a muscle in his left foot during the playoffs and was hobbling. Don Nelson was another graybeard off the bench. Like the Celtics teams of the late '60s, they were frank in discussing it. "One of these nights," Silas warned, "we're going to reach back and nothing's going to be there."

Television, specifically CBS, had stretched the playoffs schedule to absurd lengths, or at least they seemed that way to the writers used to wrapping up the pro basketball season in May. The conference finals ended on Tuesday May 18, but the championship round didn't begin until Sunday the 23rd. The second game came four nights later, then the third the following Sunday. "These games are like a bad joke," Heinsohn quipped. "You keep waiting for the punch line."

In reality, the Boston coach couldn't complain much. The time off helped Havlicek's hurt left foot to heal somewhat, although it troubled him throughout the Finals.

The series at first appeared headed toward the predicted sweep. After all, the Suns hadn't beaten the Celtics since December 1974. Boston won the first game at home, 98-87, a surprisingly flat affair in which the Suns shot only 38 percent from the floor. "If felt more like January than May," Silas told the writers afterward. "It didn't seem like a playoff game."

Then the Celtics took the second in a rout, 105-90, after Boston went on a 20-2 run in the third quarter. "This team is like a swiss watch, a bunch of different parts working together," White said afterward. Scott, always thought of as an offensive prima donna, had hounded Sobers like a madman. So much so, in fact, that Scott fouled out of the first two games. Whenever he went to the bench, backup Kevin Stacom took up where he left off, harassing Sobers to the point of explosion. In the frontcourt, Cowens was doing a similar number on Adams. And when Cowens took a breather, backup center Jim Ard was there in Adams' face.

Afterward, the Phoenix papers ran a story suggesting that the Beantown boys were controlling the series because Cowens, Ard and Silas were being allowed to play rough. The Boston coaches countered by alleging that the Suns coaching staff had "planted" the stories.

"Every team cries about the same

Tied at 2-2, the series returned to Boston that Friday night for a nationally televised game that treated the country to the NBA's best and worst, all wrapped in one three-overtime package.

thing," White told reporters. "Look, if you let a team do all they want to do, they're going to crush you. But stop them, and they get mad."

White himself faced off with Westphal, which was a rematch of their battle two years earlier for the starting job in Boston. "I know his moves from the knock-down, drag-out practices we had," White said. He had used that knowledge to stifle the Suns' scoring leader in Game 1. Westphal had responded with 17 points in the first half of Game 2, but then White shut him down again in the second half.

The Suns stepped up their intensity for Game 3, played at Veterans Memorial Coliseum on Sunday morning to accommodate television (Suns' general manager Jerry Colangelo would later apologize to local clergy for the early tipoff time). Boston didn't score for nearly five minutes at the outset of the second period and trailed 33-17 at one point. Then Sobers and Stacom

got into a fistfight, and both were ejected.

"We can't let them bully us," Sobers explained afterward.

"It was rough," agreed Van Arsdale. "but that's how Boston likes to play. I almost got my head taken off one time."

Boston began to charge back in the third and cut a lead that had once been 23 points down to two with three minutes left in the game. At that point, Adams came alive. He drove for two buckets, hit Westphal going to the hoop for another, then tipped in a Westphal miss moments later.

That was enough to get Phoenix a win, 105-98. Adams finished with 33 points and 14 rebounds. Both Scott and Cowens had fouled out, Scott for the third straight game, which left the Boston coaching staff fussing that the officials had been influenced by the media. The Celtics also picked up two technicals.

"The newspaper beat us," Heinsohn lamented. "I didn't know the power of the press was that big. We were lucky to run up and down the floor. That was hometown cooking. That's what it was."

"We're still 2-1," Cowens said confidently. "I ain't worried. We'll get 'er. If we don't get 'er today. We'll get 'er tomorrow."

As expected, the officials made their statement in Game 4 on Wednesday June 2. Refs Don Murphy and Manny Sokol whistled 21 fouls in the first 10 minutes. Heinsohn responded by raging and stomping and fussing on the sideline and claimed later that the affair was pure "high school."

Havlicek and Cowens, though, called it straight up and said the Celtics had persisted in stupid fouls. Even so, the game was anybody's to steal. With 90 seconds left, Sobers took the ball down the middle and hit a bank shot that put the Suns up by four. Still, Boston had a chance to tie but lost 109-107 when White missed a late jumper.

Tied at 2-2, the series returned to Boston that Friday night for a nationally televised game that treated the country to the NBA's best and worst, all wrapped in one three-overtime package.

"That was the most exciting basketball game I've ever seen," recalled Rick Barry, who worked the event as part of the CBS broadcast crew. "They just had one great play after another. I'll never forget the end. JoJo White was so exhausted, he just sat down on the court. It was such an emotional and physical game for everybody involved."

It didn't exactly begin as a classic, though. After nine minutes, Boston was up, 32-12. The Celtics went on to score 38 points in the first quarter and seemed on the verge of eclipsing the Suns. But Phoenix stayed in it somehow, cutting a 22-point deficit to 15 by the half. Then the Suns went to their defense and held Boston to a mere 34 points over the last two quarters of regulation. The two teams came down to a tight close. Perry missed two free throws for Phoenix, and Havlicek did the same for Boston. Regulation ended at 95-all.

The first overtime brought six more points for each team and a controversy for the ages. With time running off the clock, Silas signalled to official Richie Powers that he wanted a Boston timeout. The Celtics had none left, and according to the rules, Powers was supposed to call a technical on Silas for taking a timeout the team didn't have. Instead, Powers ignored Silas. The official later explained that he didn't want to see the game end on such a call. The Suns coaches were incensed. Barry, in the broadcast booth, was incensed, too.

"Richie Powers flat out didn't want the Celtics to lose like that," Barry said in a recent interview. "He said so later. Silas was right in his face. But Powers chose to ignore him. And that's horrible. Unbelievable."

The controversy only grew with the second overtime. With 15 seconds left, the Celtics owned a three-point lead, 109-106, and the Garden was rocking with chants of "We're Number One." But at that point, the teams took turns matching miracles. First, Van Arsdale scored for Phoenix. Then Westphal got a steal, but Perry

Havlicek, the '76 MVP.

missed with a 14-foot jumper. He rebounded and scored on the second effort to put the Suns up, 110-109. With four seconds left, the Celtics raced back upcourt, where Havlicek motored along the left side, cut toward the hoop, stopped and shoved up a 15-foot bank shot. When it fell through, the Garden erupted. The Celtics celebrated as hundreds of fans rushed onto the floor, overwhelming the Garden's elderly and understaffed security force. A table was overturned and general mayhem prevailed, while Powers tried to get both coaches' attention.

The official ruled that one second remained on the clock, which took some time for the public address announcer to communicate to the crowd. Eventually, the security staff got the floor cleared, and play was

set to resume. Phoenix would have to go the length of the floor to score with only a second remaining.

But during the delay Westphal had come up with an idea. Why not call a timeout, which the Suns didn't have? The officials would have to call a technical. The Celtics would get a free throw, but under the rules of the day the Suns would get the ball at halfcourt with a shot to tie.

MacLeod agreed, and this time the officials called the technical. White hit the free throw, giving the Celtics a 112-110 lead.

Then, as the hour neared midnight, the Suns went to Gar Heard on the inbounds. He arched a high shot that swished, leaving the Celtics floored.

With the score tied at 112, incredibly, the game headed into a third overtime.

With most of his prime-timers on the bench with six fouls, Heinsohn went rummaging among his troops to find someone to play. He settled on little-used Glenn McDonald, a 6'6" forward who had been the team's number one draft pick out of Long Beach State in 1974. His NBA-career would last just nine more games after the 1976 Finals. He would be released in the 1976-77 season by Milwuakee. But for five minutes of the third overtime, McDonald had the basketball world's attention. He scored six points, the last two on a short jumper to give Boston a 128-126 win.

The Suns had gotten nothing for their effort except bruises. Afterward they were more defiant than ever. "We know we're going to beat them," Heard declared. "It's going to take seven now, but we know we're going to beat them. We showed we came to play."

Trailing 3-2, the Suns headed home for Game 6 on Sunday June 6. There, they traded hand checks with the Celtics in a defensive struggle. Each team scored 20 in the first, then Boston scored 18 in the second while holding the Suns to 13. Erickson had attempted to play at the start of the second, but reinjured his sprained ankle and never returned. After falling behind by 11, Phoenix moved even

Cowens still helps out. Here he works with Stojko.

1973-74 BOSTON CELTICS

SEATED (left to right) -- Jo Jo White, Don Chaney, Captain John Havlicek, President Red Auerbach
Chairman Bob Schmertz, Coach Tom Heinsohn, Dave Cowens, Paul Silas, Asst. Coach John Killilea.
STANDING (left to right) -- Asst. Trainer Mark Volk, Dr. Sam Kane, Paul Westphal, Phil Hankinson
Steve Downing, Don Nelson, Hank Finkel, Steve Kuberski, Art Williams, Dr. Tom Silva, Trainer
Frank Challant.

The 1974 champions.

again in the third and actually took a 67-66 lead on a Sobers' free throw with 7:25 left in the game.

But Cowens, Havlicek and Scott took control from there. Havlicek hit two free throws, then Cowens stole the ball, drove, scored and drew the foul. He then made the extra shot for the three-point play. After that, Cowens scored two baskets and Havlicek another to put it away.

During the run, Phoenix's only response was four free throws. The Celtics rode this surge to an 87-80 win and their thirteenth championship.

"We had to gut it out all the way," Heinsohn told the gathering of writers. "Phoenix has a fine team with a great shooter. When the game was up for

grabs, it was a question of pure guts. Everyone was tired, but our guys have been there before and did it."

Much of the Boston run had been fueled by Charlie Scott's three steals. He also scored nine points in the fourth period, finishing the game with 25 points and 11 rebounds. The outburst shoved him out of an 11-for-44 shooting slump through the first five games of the series. In all five he had fouled out.

White scored 15 on the afternoon and led Boston throughout the series with 130 points in six games. For that performance, he was named the series MVP. "Our offense really wasn't that great," White said. "But defense will do it for you every time, and our defense did it."

Adams scored 20 and Sobers 19 for the Suns. "Our players felt they would win today," said an obviously disappointed MacLeod. "But Boston drove us out of our patterns. But certainly nobody has to be embarrassed about being associated with the Phoenix Suns anymore."

For the eighth time in his career, Havlicek had a go at the champagne. "You get yourself so worked up psychologically and physically that you wonder at times if it's really worth it," he said. "But after it's over, it feels like 15,000 years lifted off your shoulders."

He was asked if winning ever got old. He took another drink.

"It never gets old," he said. "It gets old only if you lose."

Pinckney closed out the season with a sizzle.

Fox, the first-round pick in '91.

Mo' Better Bench

F ilmmaker Spike Lee explained it best in his film *Mo' Better Blues.* "Just what is 'Mo' better'?" one of Lee's character's inquired.

"Mo' better is mo' better," was the answer.

The same could be said for the Celtics' bench heading into the 1991-92 season. After years of being maligned for not providing enough support for the starting five, Boston's bench is both more and better. Nobody has a keener understanding of this than guard Reggie Lewis, who served an apprenticeship as a reserve in 1987-88.

"Back in 1988 there were only about six guys that were playing, and we were known for not having a bench," Lewis said. "Now we have a bench, and the guys are playing and contributing."

The obvious parts of this equation are sixth-man Kevin McHale and third-guard Dee Brown. But there are many mo' factors, and that makes things better for Boston.

There's forward Ed Pinckney, who had an outstanding spring last season and finished off the year with a strong performance in the playoffs. For the season, Pinckney averaged nearly five rebounds (2.2 of them were offensive) while playing just 16 minutes per game. He also shot a career-high .897 from the free-throw line. But Pinckney's real show came in the playoffs when through

A.J. Wynder came up from the CBA.

Kleine is a solid backup center.

Kleine has developed offensively.

11 games he shot .762 (16 of 21) from the floor.

"Pinckney played very well in the playoffs," said Celtics' president Red Auerbach. "In fact, the last three months of the season he played well."

Beyond Pinckney, there's solid, dependable back-up center Joe Kleine, whose availability pushes the bench to nine deep. At the end of last season, that number ran to 10 deep once Dereck Smith became available. His status for '91-92 is uncertain after offseason knee surgery, but the Celtics would love to have this tough, experienced player back in uniform.

At guard, there are a host of candidates vying for a roster spot. Coming off the injured list is veteran John Bagley. Then there's last season's late acquisition, A.J. Wynder, and this season's first-round draft pick, Rick Fox out of the University of North Carolina.

And in August, the team signed Anderson Hunt, the fine rookie free agent out of Nevada-Las Vegas.

In the frontcourt are 7'2" center Stojko Vrankovic from Yugoslavia, 6'10" forward Michael Smith and free agent forward Dave Popson.

Camp will reveal which players earn the 11th and 12th roster spots. The pressure will be a bit high as this crowd competes for a job. Once those decisions are made, and the regular season brings a new round of pressure. Rather than deep heat, it's a slow cooker. At times, fans fail to

Stojko has starred in his native Yugoslavia.

Pinckney's specialty is the offensive board.

understand the special difficulties faced by bench players. "Sometimes when you're not playing, you tend to get down on yourself," Pinckney said. "It's very discouraging when you don't have a chance to play. When you come to the arena on game nights, sometimes it's tough to prepare."

But keeping focused in a positive frame of mind is an important skill to master, Pinckney added. "Since I've been here I've always worked hard. I've never really given up. Every time that there was an opportunity to play, I tried to play as hard as I could. And then when the game was over, I usually tried to stay after and work on my own. I think they've respected that. When I played well in practice, they gave me a shot to play in the game."

Lewis adopted just such a strategy when he was a rookie back in 1987-88, and it paid off. Given his opportunity, he was ready to play. And that is the nature of the process. Mo' better bench becomes mo' better players.

Smith has proven he can score.

CELTICS PROFILES

LARRY BIRD

Birthdate: December 7, 1956
Birthplace: West Baden, IN
High School: Springs Valley (French Lick, IN)
College: Indiana State '79
Height: 6-9
Weight: 220
NBA Experience: 12 Years

HOW ACQUIRED: Celtics first-round draft choice in 1978... 6th pick overall.

1990-91 SEASON: His brilliance was once again displayed as he finished in the top ten in free throw percentage (10th) and 3-point field goal percentage (8th) despite a season which saw him miss 22 games with injury (team went 10-12)... missed 7 games from 4/6-4/19 due to back spasms, returned to play 34 minutes in the season finale against Atlanta... on 3/31: 52 minutes vs. Chicago, 34 points (15-36, 1-5, 3-3), 15 rebounds, 8 assists and 3 blocks; had 9 points in the 2nd OT (4-5, 1-1) after 0-5 fgs in the 1st OT - 36 fga tied a career high while 34 points was a personal high since 2/27 when he scored 35 points vs. Minnesota... ended the season by making 38 of 91 (.418) from 3-point land over his last 20 games... vs. Milwaukee on 11/13, he was held to 5 points, a personel low in a non-injury related or ejection-related game since 1/2/81 (0 pts at GS)... played in his 800th career game on 11/16 vs. Utah... achieved his 5,000th career assist on 11/14 vs Charlotte, and became the 15th player to total 20,000 points on 11/30 vs. Washington; became the 5th NBA player to reach both those numbers (Jabbar, Robertson, West and Havlicek)... scored 43 points on 12/5, the most ever by any player in a Celtics-Nuggets game... 4-4 3-pt fgs vs. Milwaukee on 12/12... selected to the All-Star game as a starter, but did not play due to a back injury which kept him from playing in 14 straight games from 1/8-2/3; played vs. Charlotte on 2/6, but did not travel to New York (2/7) based on decision by team's medical staff... 4-6 3-pt fgs at GS on 2/14 and vs. Minnesota on 2/27... 35 points vs. Minnesota on 2/27 was the most ever by a Celtic vs. the Wolves... 5-8 3-pt fgs vs. Portland on 3/3... tied a personal and team record by making 7 3-pt fgs (10 attempts) vs. Indiana in Hartford on 3/4... 5-8 3-pt fgs vs. Miami on 3/6... 10+ mins 60 times... 20+ mins 55 times... 30+ mins 55 times... 40+ mins 25 times... 50+ mins 2 times ... 10+ pts 55 times... 20+ pts 27 times (team is 24-3)... 30+ pts 5 times... 40+ pts 2 times... 10+ rebs 20 times... 10+ assts 17 times... 30 double-doubles... 3 triple-doubles... 0 to's/30+ mins 2 times... ended the season with 20,883 career points finishing as the 13th best all-time top scorer... **1991 Playoffs:** became Boston's all-time playoff scoring leader... registered a triple-double in Game One vs. Indiana... in Game Five clincher vs. Indiana, he made a Superman-like return after a serious fall to the floor earlier in the game; had a game high 32 points and sparked a key 39-25 run... missed Game One loss vs. Detroit due to back spasms... was inhibited throughout the playoffs by the back injury, and had surgery on June 7th for a ruptured L4-5; he had congenital stenosis of the foramen where the L5 nerve root exited and he had a problem with rotational and transational instability of the spine - the two hour surgery included the removal of the disc, large fragment which was teased from a bed of scar, and the nerve root was freed out.

PROFESSIONAL CAREER: Drafted by Boston on the first-round of the 1978 draft, as a junior eligible, the 6th pick overall... voted the NBA Rookie of the Year in 1980 and was a member of the league's All-Rookie Team... a member of the All-NBA First Team his first nine years, and to the Second Team in his 11th... named to the all-star team 11 times... named the all-star game MVP in 1982... All-Defensive Second Team in 1982, 1983, and 1986... playoff MVP in 1984 and 1986... regular season MVP in 1984, 1985, and 1986; one of only three players in NBA history to achieve the feat in three consecutive seasons... Player of the Week 15 times... Player of the Month 7 times... NBA ft% leader in 1984, 1986, 1987, and 1990... Boston has never had a r/s losing month with him in the line-up... whenver he plays 3,000 minutes, Boston advances to the NBA Finals; whenever he doesn't, Boston does not advance... only Celtic to score 2,000+ points in three consecutive seasons... 68 triple-doubles, including 58 in the r/s... 40+ points 51 times, 46 in the r/s... 50+ pts 4 times, all in the r/s... was held scoreless on 1/3/81 at Golden State... set NBA playoff record for most points in one year, 1984... tallied 34 points in Game Five win over the Lakers in the 1984 Finals, despite 97 degree temperatures inside Boston Garden... scored 10,000th career point on 1/11/85 vs. Washington... consecutive game-winning buzzer beaters on 1/27/85 (Portland) and 1/29/85 (Detroit)... set team mark with 60 pts on 3/12/85... named AP Male Athlete of the Year for 1986... named The Sporting News Man of the Year for 1986... won the long distance shootout in the first three years of its existence... triple-double in 1986 title clincher vs. Houston... consecutive 40+ point games on 3/20/87 (Seattle) and 3/22/87 (New Jersey)... achieved a triple-double at halftime on 4/1/87 vs. Washington... on 5/23/87, was ejected with Bill Laimbeer for fighting... made miraculous steal of Isiah Thomas' inbounds pass with five seconds left to give Boston a win in Game Five of their 1987 playoff series... on 11/7/87 at Wash, game-tying 3-pt fg with 4 secs left in reg; hit game-winner with 0 secs left in OT... on 11/11/87, he registered Boston's first 40/20 game (42 points and 20 rebs) vs. Indiana... on 5/22/88, in 7th game win vs. Hawks, scored 34 points including 20 (9-10 fgs) in the 4th... first player in NBA history to register 50% fgs and 90% fts in the same season, and he is the only player to do it twice... missed all but six games in the 1988-89 season due to surgical removal of bone spurs in both heels... had the second best (Calvin Murphy, 78) free throw streak in NBA annals snapped at 71 on 2/13/90 in Houston.

COLLEGE CAREER: Consensus All-America in 1978 and 1979 and The Sporting News Player of the Year in 1979... TSN All-America First Team in 1978 and 1979... graduated as the fifth all-time leading NCAA scorer (30.3 ppg)... ISU compiled a record of 81-13 overall and 50-1 at home in his three years... led ISU to the 1979 NCAA Finals... John Wooden Award winner in 1979... also attended Indiana University, and Northwood Institute, but did not play.

PERSONAL: Larry Joe Bird is married to the former Dinah Mattingly... has four brothers and one sister, mother's name is Georgia... brother Eddie plays basketball at ISU... avid outdoorsman... likes Kenny Rogers' music... fan of the St. Louis Cardinals... most memorable Christmas: all, because of family... returns to Indiana during the summer... owns "Larry Bird's Boston Connection," a hotel/restaurant in Terre Haute... on 8/2/84, a street in Terre Haute was named in his honor... holds the annual "Larry Bird Pro All-Star Scholarship Classic" during the off-season in Indiana... shoe size is 13 and a half.

TOP REGULAR SEASON PERFORMANCES

Points
60 vs. Atl. at N.O. (3-12-85)
53 vs. Indiana (3-30-83)
50 at Dallas (3-10-86)
50 vs. Atlanta (11-10-89)
49 vs. Washington (1-27-88)
49 at Phoenix (2-15-88)

Rebounds
21 at Washington (3-16-82)
21 at Denver (12-29-81)
21 at LA Lakers (2-11-81)
21 at Philadelphia (11-1-80)
20 six times

Assists
17 at Golden State (2-16-84)
16 vs. Cleveland (3-21-90)
15 vs. Washington (4-1-87)
15 vs. Cleveland (3-27-85)
15 vs. Atlanta (1-13-82)
15 vs. Cleveland (11-2-90)

NBA RECORD

Year	Team	G	Min	FGM	FGA	Pct	FTM	FTA	Pct	Off	Def	Tot	Ast	PF-Dq	St	Bl	Pts	Avg
79-80	Bos.	82	2955	693	1463	.474	301	360	.836	216	636	852	370	279-4	143	53	1745	21.3
80-81	Bos.	82	3239	719	1503	.478	283	328	.863	191	704	895	451	239-2	161	63	1741	21.2
81-82	Bos.	77	2923	711	1414	.503	328	380	.863	200	637	837	447	244-0	143	66	1761	22.9
82-83	Bos.	79	2982	747	1481	.504	351	418	.840	193	677	870	458	197-0	148	71	1867	23.6
83-84	Bos.	79	3028	758	1542	.492	374	421	.888	181	615	796	520	197-0	144	69	1908	24.2
84-85	Bos.	80	3161	918	1760	.522	403	457	.882	164	678	842	531	208-0	129	98	2295	28.7
85-86	Bos.	82	3113	796	1606	.496	441	492	.896	190	615	805	557	182-0	166	51	2115	25.8
86-87	Bos.	74	3005	786	1497	.525	414	455	.910	124	558	682	566	185-3	135	70	2076	28.1
87-88	Bos.	76	2965	881	1672	.527	415	453	.916	108	595	703	467	157-0	125	57	2275	29.9
88-89	Bos.	6	189	49	104	.471	18	19	.947	1	36	37	29	18-0	6	5	116	19.3
89-90	Bos.	75	2944	718	1517	.473	319	343	.930	90	622	712	562	173-2	106	61	1820	24.3
90-91	Bos.	60	2277	462	1017	.454	163	183	.891	53	456	509	431	118-0	108	58	1164	19.4
TOTALS:		852	32781	8238	16576	.497	3810	4309	.884	1711	6829	8540	5389	2197-11	1154	722	20883	24.5

Three-Point Field Goals: 1979-80, 58-for-143 (.406); 1980-81, 20-for-74 (.270); 1981-82, 11-for-52 (.212); 1982-83, 22-for-77 (.286); 1983-84, 18-for-73 (.247); 1984-85, 56-for-131 (.427); 1985-86, 82-for-194 (.423); 1986-87, 90-for-225 (.400); 1987-88, 98-for-237 (.414); 1988-89, 0-for-0 (.000); 1989-90, 65-for-195 (.333); 1990-91, 77-for-198 (.389). Totals: 597-for-1599 (.373).

PLAYOFF RECORD

Year	Team	G	Min	FGM	FGA	Pct	FTM	FTA	Pct	Off	Def	Tot	Ast	PF-Dq	St	Bl	Pts	Avg
79-80	Bos.	9	372	83	177	.469	22	25	.880	22	79	101	42	30-0	14	8	192	21.3
80-81	Bos.	17	750	147	313	.470	76	85	.894	49	189	238	103	53-0	39	17	373	21.9
81-82	Bos.	12	490	88	206	.427	37	45	.822	33	117	150	67	43-0	23	17	214	17.8
82-83	Bos.	6	240	49	116	.422	24	29	.828	20	55	75	41	15-0	13	3	123	20.5
83-84	Bos.	23	961	229	437	.524	167	190	.879	62	190	252	136	71-0	54	27	632	27.5
84-85	Bos.	20	815	196	425	.461	121	136	.890	53	129	182	115	54-0	34	19	520	26.0
85-86	Bos.	18	770	171	331	.517	101	109	.927	34	134	168	148	55-0	37	11	466	25.9
86-87	Bos.	23	1015	216	454	.476	176	193	.912	41	190	231	165	55-1	27	19	622	27.0
87-88	Bos.	17	763	152	338	.450	101	113	.894	29	121	150	115	45-0	36	14	417	24.5
88-89	Bos.	0	0	0	0	.000	0	0	.000	0	0	0	0	0-0	0	0	0	0.0
89-90	Bos.	5	207	44	99	.444	29	32	.906	7	39	46	44	10-0	5	5	122	24.4
90-91	Bos.	10	396	62	152	.408	44	51	.863	8	64	72	65	28-0	13	3	171	17.1
TOTALS:		160	6779	1437	3048	.471	898	1008	.891	358	1307	1665	1041	459-1	295	143	3852	24.1

Three-Point Field Goals: 1979-80, 4-for-15 (.267); 1980-81, 3-for-8 (.375); 1981-82, 1-for-6 (.167); 1982-83, 1-for-4 (.250); 1983-84, 7-for-17 (.412); 1984-85, 7-for-25 (.280); 1985-86, 23-for-56 (.411), 1986-87, 14-for-41 (.341); 1987-88, 12-for-32 (.375); 1988-89, 0-for-0 (.000); 1989-90, 5-for-19 (.263); 1990-91, 3-for-21 (.143). Totals: 80-for-244 (.328).

ALL STAR GAME RECORD

Year	Team	Min	FGM	FGA	Pct	FTM	FTA	Pct	Off	Def	Tot	Ast	PF-Dq	St	Bl	Pts	Avg
1980	Bos.	23	3	6	.500	0	0	.000	3	3	6	7	1-0	1	0	7	7.0
1981	Bos.	18	1	5	.200	0	0	.000	1	3	4	10	1-0	1	0	2	2.0
1982	Bos.	28	7	12	.583	5	8	.625	0	12	12	5	3-0	1	1	19	19.0
1983	Bos.	29	7	14	.500	0	0	.000	3	10	13	7	4-0	2	0	14	14.0
1984	Bos.	33	6	18	.333	4	4	1.000	1	6	7	3	1-0	2	0	16	16.0
1985	Bos.	31	8	16	.500	5	6	.833	5	3	8	2	3-0	0	1	21	21.0
1986	Bos.	35	8	18	.444	5	6	.833	2	6	8	5	5-0	7	0	23	23.0
1987	Bos.	35	7	18	.389	4	4	1.000	2	4	6	5	5-0	2	0	18	18.0
1988	Bos.	32	2	8	.250	2	2	1.000	0	7	7	1	4-0	4	1	6	6.0
1990	Bos.	23	3	8	.375	2	2	1.000	2	6	8	3	1-0	3	0	8	8.0
1991	Bos. selected, did not play due to back injury																
TOTALS:		287	52	123	.423	27	32	.844	19	60	79	41	28-0	23	3	134	13.4

Three-Point Field Goals: 1980, 1-for-2 (.500); 1983, 0-for-1 (.000); 1985, 0-for-1 (.000); 1986, 2-for-4 (.500); 1987, 0-for-3 (.000); 1988, 0-for-1 (.000); 1990, 0-for-1 (.000). Totals: 3-for-13 (.231).

SEASON/CAREER HIGHS

	FGM	FGA	FTM	FTA	REB	AST	ST	BL	PTS
1990-91/Regular Season	18/22	36/36	12/15	13/17	15/21	15/17	6/9	5/5	45/60
1991/Playoffs	12/17	20/33	9/14	10/15	12/21	12/16	3/6	2/4	32/43

DEE BROWN

Birthdate: November 29,1968
Birthplace: Jacksonville, FL
High School: Bolles High (FL)
College: Jacksonville '90
Height: 6-1
Weight: 161
Years Pro: 1 Year

HOW ACQUIRED: Celtics first-round draft choice in 1990... 19th pick overall.

1990-91 SEASON: The Celtics 1990 top draft pick was among the first-year elite in the NBA, and was named to the 1991 NBA All-Rookie Team compiling the third highest point total behind Derrick Coleman and Lionel Simmons... gained instant notoriety by winning the Gatorade Slam Dunk Championship during the all-star weekend in Charlotte... started 5 times, team went 3-2; his numbers as a starter were 202 minutes, 71 points (30-63, 11-13), 18 rebounds, and 33 assists... ended March by making 10 of 12 fgs vs. Chicago on 3/31, concluding a fabulous month; in 16 games, he tallied 205 (12.8) points (86-173, 1-10, 32-37), 77 (4.8) assists and 493 (30.8) minutes... started 3 times in Brian Shaw's absence (3/4-3/8) and including the 3/3 game when Shaw was injured, the rookie totalled 162 minutes, 67 points (28-48, 0-3, 11-14) and 26 assists in 4 games... totalled 7 straight 10+ point outings from 12/23-1/8... in 17 games from 11/30-1/4: 61-109 fgs (.560), including 21-29 (.724) over the first 5 games... his fg% after 12/14: .556 (60-108)... in 3 Hartford games: 17-24 (.708) fgs... dished out 19 assists in 2 games vs. Portland... 10+ mins 79 times... 20+ mins 58 times (including 20 straight from 2/22-3/31)... 30+ mins 19 times... 40+ mins 5 times... 10+ pts 36 times... 20+ pts 3 times... 10+ assts once... 1 double-double... **1991 Playoffs:** was outstanding against Detroit, averaging 15.8 points in 31.5 minutes... in Game Two vs. Detroit, he tallied 15 fourth quarter points (22 overall) in a must-win situation... in Game Three vs. Detroit, he contributed 13 points, 9 rebounds, and 6 assists in 29 minutes.
COLLEGE CAREER: Played 21 games as a freshman, started once... moved into the starting lineup for 23 games as a sophomore, mainly at shooting guard... led Jacksonville in steals (46) and free throw shooting (.818), and ranked second in scoring with 10.1 ppg... named to the All-SBC Second Team as a junior, starting all 30 games; played predominantly at small forward... led the Dolphins in scoring (19.6 ppg), rebounding (7.6 rpg) and steals (56)... started 16 games at point guard and 13 at small forward as a senior as he averaged 19.3 points, 5.0 assists, and 6.6 rebounds per game... finished as ninth all-time scorer in school history with 1,503 points, and finished second behind Ronnie Murphy on all-time steals list with 201... set team record for career three-pointers made with 87... field goal percentage and assists total increased each season... best season statistically was as a junior, as he posted highs in games, free throws made, free throws attempted, free throw percentage, rebounds, points, and points per game... set Sun Belt Conference Tournament record with 41 points in quarterfinal game vs. Old Dominion... named to the All-SBC First Team, and to the All-Tournament team at the Orlando All-Star Classic in April, 1990.

PERSONAL: DeCovan Kadell Brown is married, wife's name is Jill... a computer whiz, he has owned one since the age of eight... has designed his own computer programs... majored in math and computer science... has a younger sister and a younger brother... lists his dad as his most influential person... favorite basketball player was Julius Erving... favorite pregame meal is spaghetti, while his favorite meal is a cheeseburger... top musical performer is Janet Jackson... lists Orlando as his preferred NBA city (outside Boston)... prime movie is "Scarface"... lists "In Living Colour" his top television show... works with the Easter Seals... enjoys watching baseball... lived in Jacksonville his entire life, before his move to Massachusetts where he lives year-round... shoe size is 14 and a half.

TOP REGULAR SEASON PERFORMANCES

Points
22 at Washington (3-15-91)
22 vs. Indiana @ Htfd (3-4-91)
21 vs. Chicago (3-31-91)
19 vs. Portland (3-3-91)

Rebounds
6 at Miami (3-28-91)
6 vs. New Jersey (4-4-91)
5 eight times

Assists
11 at Portland (3-10-91)
9 vs. Orlando (1-30-91)
8 seven times

NBA RECORD

Year	Team	G	Min	FGM	FGA	Pct.	FTM	FTA	Pct.	Off	Def	Tot	Ast	PF-Dq	St	Bl	Pts	Avg
90-91	Bos.	82	1945	284	612	.464	137	157	.873	41	141	182	344	161-0	83	14	712	8.7

Three-Point Field Goals: 1990-91, 7-for-34 (.206).

PLAYOFF RECORD

90-91	Bos.	11	284	53	108	.491	28	34	.824	9	36	45	41	32-0	11	6	134	12.2

Three-Point Field Goals: 1990-91, 0-for-5 (.000)

SEASON/CAREER HIGHS

	FGM	FGA	FTM	FTA	REB	AST	ST	BL	PTS
1990-91/Regular Season	10/10	17/17	8/8	9/9	6/6	11/11	3/3	2/2	22/22
1991/Playoffs	9/9	14/14	8/8	10/10	9/9	10/10	2/2	1/1	22/22

KEVIN GAMBLE

Birthdate: November 13, 1965
Birthplace: Springfield, IL
High School: Lanphier High (IL)
College: Iowa '87
Height: 6-5
Weight: 210
NBA Experience: 4 Years

HOW ACQUIRED: Signed as a free agent on December 15, 1988.

1990-91 SEASON: Went from a DNP-CD in a pair of last season's five playoff games to the winner of the 1991 SportsChannel/Texaco Celtics Sixth Star Award given to the player who best represents Celtics pride... established career highs in most categories and in some cases his final numbers doubled his previous totals... season was punctuated with a career high 33-point night in Philadelphia on 4/18 (15-25, 0-1, 3-4), snapping the 32-point night (16-20 fgs) he had on 2/7 at New York... made 22 straight free throws, snapped on 4/18... a premiere field goal shooter, he led that category from 3/14-3/20 and finished 3rd in the NBA behind Portland's Buck Williams and teammate Robert Parish... fg% was as high as .625, at the all-star break... in the last 29 games before the all-star break, he made 223 of 337 fgs (.662)... made 14 of 16 shots in a 3 game span from 3/10-3/13... had a hot start, as a reserve, by making 13 of 16 (.813) fgs in the season's opening weekend... made 37 of 53 (.698) fgs in 4 games vs Charlotte... made 43 of 62 (.694) fgs in 5 games vs. New York... in a 3 game spread from 1/11-1/16, he compiled 75 points (31-49, 13-16)... started 4 times at guard (11/16, 12/23, 1/12, 2/22)... 10+ mins 82 times... 20+ mins 79 times... 30+ mins 57 times... 40+ mins 16 times... 10+ pts 67 times... 20+ pts 23 times... 30+ pts 2 times... one double-double... 10+ rebs once... **1991 Playoffs:** was one of three Celtics to start all 11 games.

PROFESSIONAL CAREER: Drafted by Portland on the third-round of the 1987 draft, the 63rd choice overall... began the 1987-88 season with the Blazers, playing nine games before being waived on December 9, 1987... joined the Quad City Thunder, and played in 40 games; he averaged 21.0 points, 5.9 rebounds, and 3.7 assists per game... finished third in the CBA Rookie of the Year voting... also played in the Phillipines with Anejo Rum... in 1988-89, he continued his play with Quad City and was the CBA's leading scorer (27.8 ppg in 12 contests) before his promotion to the Celtics... had a great stretch in the last six games of 1988-89 in which he averaged 22.8 ppg; in 6 starts, he had 137 points (57-87, 0-4, 23-30) in 235 minutes while adding 29 assists and 28 rebounds... had 10 starts in 1989-90.

COLLEGE CAREER: Played two years at Lincoln College in Lincoln, Illinois, and averaged 20.9 ppg... transferred to the University of Iowa, averaged 11.9 points and shot 54.4 percent from the field as a senior... played at Iowa under George Raveling and Tom Davis.

PERSONAL: Kevin Douglas Gamble is single... affectionately nicknamed "Oscar"... received an Associate's Degree in Law Enforcement... names Kareem Abdul-Jabbar as the greatest player he has ever seen... lists shopping, playing video games, golfing and fishing as his interests... favorite foods are spaghetti and chili, and pasta is his favorite pregame meal... enjoys the television show "Alf"... likes rap music... most influential person in his basketball life was Al Pickering, coach at Lincoln JC... names his mom as the most influential person in his private life... returns to Illinois in the summer... childhood hero is Doctor J... three people he'd most like to meet are Stevie Wonder, Nelson Mandela, and any rap star... shoe size is 14.

TOP REGULAR SEASON PERFORMANCES

Points
33 at Philadelphia (4-18-91)
32 at New York (2-7-91)
31 vs. Charlotte (4-23-89)
28 two times

Rebounds
10 at Charlotte (2-1-91)
9 at Orlando (4-6-91)
8 vs. Golden State (1-16-91)
7 three times

Assists
10 vs. Cleveland (4-14-89)
9 vs. Charlotte (11-14-90)
7 at Charlotte (4-17-89)
7 at Charlotte (12-20-90)

NBA RECORD

Year	Team	G	Min	FGM	FGA	Pct	FTM	FTA	Pct	Off	Def	Tot	Ast	PF-Dq	St	Bl	Pts	Avg
87-88	Por.	9	19	0	3	.000	0	0	.000	2	1	3	1	2-0	2	0	0	0.0
88-89	Bos.	44	375	75	136	.551	35	55	.636	11	31	42	34	40-0	14	3	187	4.3
89-90	Bos.	71	990	137	301	.455	85	107	.704	42	70	112	119	77-1	28	8	362	5.1
90-91	Bos.	82	2706	548	933	.587	185	227	.815	85	182	267	256	237-6	100	34	1281	15.6
TOTALS:		206	4090	760	1373	.554	305	389	.792	140	284	424	410	356-7	144	45	1830	8.9

Three-Point Field Goals: 1987-88, 0-for-1 (.000); 1988-89, 2-for-11 (.182); 1989-90, 3-for-18 (.167); 1990-91, 0-for-7 (.000).
Totals: 5-for-37 (.135).

PLAYOFF RECORD

Year	Team	G	Min	FGM	FGA	Pct	FTM	FTA	Pct	Off	Def	Tot	Ast	PF-Dq	St	Bl	Pts	Avg
88-89	Bos.	1	29	4	11	.364	0	2	.000	1	0	1	2	1-0	1	0	8	8.0
89-90	Bos.	3	8	3	5	.600	0	0	.000	1	0	1	2	1-0	0	0	6	2.0
90-91	Bos.	11	238	29	60	.483	8	12	.667	3	10	13	19	24-0	4	2	66	6.0
TOTALS:		15	275	36	76	.474	8	14	.571	5	10	15	23	26-0	5	2	80	5.3

Three-Point Field Goals: 1988-89, 0-for-1 (.000).
Totals: 0-for-1 (.000).1990-91

SEASON/CAREER HIGHS

	FGM	FGA	FTM	FTA	REB	AST	ST	BL	PTS
1990-91/Regular Season	16/16	25/25	8/9	9/12	10/10	9/10	5/5	3/3	33/33
1991/Playoffs	8/8	13/13	3/3	4/4	4/4	5/5	2/2	1/1	18/18

JOE KLEINE

Birthdate: January 4, 1962
Birthplace: Colorado Springs, CO
High School: Slater High (Slater, MO)
College: Arkansas '85
Height: 7-0
Weight: 271
NBA Experience: 6 Years

HOW ACQUIRED: Traded by Sacramento with Ed Pinckney to Boston for Danny Ainge and Brad Lohaus on February 23, 1989.

1990-91 SEASON: Concluded his second full season with Boston after being acquired with Ed Pinckney from Sacramento on 2/23/89 for Danny Ainge (now with Portland) and Brad Lohaus (now with Milwaukee)... played in 53 of Boston's first 56 games, the exceptions were one due to an injury (dizzyness from a fall) suffered on opening night vs. Cleveland which caused him to miss the road opener on 11/3 at New York, and two DNP-CD against Philadelphia (12/1 and 12/19)... longest stretch of consecutive action was 32 games from 12/20-2/27... played in 6 straight games from 3/17-3/29, tallying 79 minutes, 13 points (6-16, 1-2), and 32 rebounds... started at Detroit on 1/21, as he registered 18 points (7-10, 4-4) in 31 minutes... 10+ mins 42 times... 20+ mins 9 times... 30+ mins once... 10+ pts 4 times... DNP-CD 9 times...
1991 Playoffs: appeared in 5 games, including a start in Game Six against Detroit due to Robert Parish's injury.

PROFESSIONAL CAREER: Drafted by Sacramento on the first-round of the 1985 draft, the sixth player taken overall... started 18 of his 80 appearances in his rookie season... played in all 82 games in 1987-88, including starts in 60... was the Kings second best rebounder in 1987-88... his minutes, field goals made, attempted, and percentage, free throws made, attempted, and percentage, offensive, defensive, and total rebounds, assists, blocks, points, and scoring average all increased in his first three years... missed just nine games in three-plus seasons with the Kings... in

1988-89, he started 11 times in 47 appearances for Sacramento... was a 92% free throw shooter in 1988-89 with Sacramento... was chosen the SportsChannel/Texaco Sixth Man of the Year for 1989-90... hit the game-winning field goal with 8.2 seconds left vs. Philadelphia on 3/11/90.

COLLEGE CAREER: Played his freshman season with Notre Dame and made 64% of his fgs (32-50)... transferred to Arkansas... sat out the entire 1981-82 season... chosen Southwest Conference Newcomer of the Year in his first season with the Razorbacks, averaging 13.3 ppg and 7.3 rpg in 1982-83... Arkansas' top scorer in his junior and senior years... ppg increased all four years... member of the 1984 US Olympic Team... member of the 1982 World University Games Team... graduated as the fourth best scorer in Arkansas' history (1,753).

PERSONAL: Joseph William Kleine and his wife Dana have one child, Daniel Christopher (2/23/89), born the day of his father's trade to Boston... college teammate of Alvin Robertson, Darrell Walker, Scott Hastings, and Tony Brown... likes to fish, golf, read and listen to country music... enjoys viewing hockey games... favorite pregame meal is spaghetti and pasta... childhood heroes are Bill Walton and Dave Cowens... helped the Massachusetts Committee for Children and Youth by appearing in a video aimed at preventing child abuse; also involved with the Leukemia Society, Big Brothers and Big Sisters, and People Reaching Out organizations... favorite television shows are "M*A*S*H" and "The Andy Griffith Show"... likes the Kansas City Royals... would like to be Celtics' booster Greg Norman for one day... would like to meet Pope John Paul II... lists Dallas (besides Boston) as his favorite NBA city... spends part of his summer in Dallas and Arkansas... names his dad as his most influential person... graduated with a degree in Business Administration... most memorable Christmas is 1989, because it was his son's first... shoe size is 16.

CAREER HIGHS: 23 points at LA Clippers (3-20-88)
23 points vs. LA Clippers (4-2-88)
18 rebounds vs. Chicago (12-3-85)
8 assists vs. LA Clippers (4-2-87)

TOP REGULAR SEASON PERFORMANCES (WITH CELTICS)

Points
18 at Atlanta (3-13-90)
18 at Detroit (1-21-91)
16 vs. Charlotte (2-7-90)
16 vs. Houston (3-31-89)

Rebounds
13 vs. Washington (1-3-90)
12 at Chicago (11-4-89)
11 vs. Orlando (4-18-90)
11 vs. Houston (3-31-89)

Assists
4 vs. Houston (3-31-89)
4 vs. Portland (3-29-89)
3 at Atlanta (4-13-89)
3 vs. Orlando (4-18-90)
3 vs. Denver (12-5-90)

NBA RECORD

Year	Team	G	Min	FGM	FGA	Pct	FTM	FTA	Pct	Off	Def	Tot	Ast	PF-Dq	St	Bl	Pts	Avg
85-86	Sac.	80	1180	160	344	.465	94	130	.723	113	260	373	46	224-1	24	34	414	5.2
86-87	Sac.	79	1658	256	543	.471	110	140	.786	173	310	483	71	213-2	35	30	622	7.9
87-88	Sac.	82	1999	324	686	.472	153	188	.814	179	400	579	93	228-1	28	59	801	9.8
88-89	Sac/Bos	75	1411	175	432	.405	134	152	.882	124	254	378	67	192-2	33	23	484	6.5
89-90	Bos.	81	1365	176	367	.480	83	100	.830	117	238	355	46	170-0	15	27	435	5.4
90-91	Bos.	72	850	102	218	.468	54	69	.783	71	173	244	21	108-0	15	14	258	3.6
TOTALS:		469	8463	1193	2590	.461	628	779	.806	777	1635	2412	344	1135-6	150	187	3014	6.4

Three-Point Field Goals: 1986-87, 0-for-1 (.000); 1988-89, 0-for-2 (.000); 1989-90, 0-for-4 (.000); 1990-91, 0-for-2 (.000).
Totals: 0-for-9 (.000).

PLAYOFF RECORD

Year	Team	G	Min	FGM	FGA	Pct	FTM	FTA	Pct	Off	Def	Tot	Ast	PF-Dq	St	Bl	Pts	Avg
85-86	Sac.	3	45	5	13	.385	5	6	.833	8	6	14	1	8-0	1	1	15	5.0
88-89	Bos.	3	65	6	11	.545	7	9	.778	4	13	17	2	9-0	0	1	19	6.3
89-90	Bos.	5	79	13	17	.765	5	6	.833	3	11	14	2	12-0	2	3	31	6.2
90-91	Bos.	5	31	4	9	.444	0	0	.000	5	6	11	1	7-0	2	0	8	1.6
TOTALS:		16	220	28	50	.560	17	21	.810	20	36	56	6	36-0	3	5	73	4.6

Three-Point Field Goals: 1988-89, 0-for-1 (.000); 1989-90, 0-for-1 (.000).
Totals: 0-for-2 (.000).

SEASON/CAREER HIGHS

	FGM	FGA	FTM	FTA	REB	AST	ST	BL	PTS
1990-91/Regular Season	7/10	10/17	5/8	6/9	8/18	3/8	2/3	1/3	18/23
1991/Playoffs	3/4	3/6	0/6	0/7	5/11	1/1	0/1	0/1	6/12

REGGIE LEWIS

Birthdate: November 21, 1965
Birthplace: Baltimore, MD
High School: Dunbar High (MD)
College: Northeastern '87
Height: 6-7
Weight: 195
NBA Experience: 4 Years

HOW ACQUIRED: Celtics first-round draft choice in 1987... 22nd pick overall.

1990-91 SEASON: Boston's top pick of 1987 had another great season... established career bests in minutes, scoring average, blocks, rebounds, and, for the fourth straight season, free throw percentage... had a career high 42 points (16-24, 10-12) on 4/12 vs. Miami... in 53 minutes on 3/31 vs. Chicago, he tallied 25 points (10-20, 1-1, 4-8) and 4 blocks; his first 3-pt fg of the season tied the game at 110 with 19.4 seconds left in the 4th quarter... collected 20+ pts in 6 of 7 games from 3/19-4/2, and totalled 162 points (69-135, 1-2, 23-33)... scored 55 points in season's opening weekend... scored the last 4 points vs. the LAC on 1/11, in 2-pt win (broke tie w/2 fts, 2.5 secs left)... had just 2 turnovers in 6 games from 2/3-2/15... missed 3 games due to injury; 2/22 vs. New Jersey due to a groin pull, and games on 4/18 and 4/19 due to back spasms... blocked a career high 5 shots vs. Washington on 3/20... had no turnovers in 3 games from 3/20-3/28... made 37 of 58 (.638) fgs in 3 games vs. Cleveland... 10+ mins 79 times... 20+ mins 78 times... 30+ mins 66 times... 40+ mins 28 times... 50+ mins once... 10+ pts 74 times (including his last 41)... 20+ pts 32 times... 30+ pts 6 times... 40+ pts once ... 10+ rebs 7 times... 7 double-doubles... 0 to's/30+ mins 12 times... **1991 Playoffs:** started all 11 games, and was Boston's leading scorer at 22.4 points per outing... led Boston in minutes played with 462... team leader with 28 points in Game One vs. Indiana; also led the club in four games against Detroit, including a 30-point outing in Game Five.

PROFESSIONAL CAREER: Drafted by Boston on the first-round of the 1987 draft, the 22nd pick overall... saw limited duty in his first NBA season... best stretch in 1987-88 was a five game span from 11/15-11/21 as he scored 49 total points... in 1988-89, he started 57 times in the small forward position, replacing the injured Larry Bird... chosen the SportsChannel Sixth Man of the Year in 1988-89... finished second to Phoenix' Kevin Johnson in the NBA's Most Improved Player voting (1988-89), as he improved his scoring average from 4.5 to 18.5 and his minute total from 405 to 2657... started 54 times in 1989-90, establishing what were career highs for his first three years in field goal shooting (.496), free throw shooting (.808), and assists (225).

COLLEGE CAREER: Four year starter at Northeastern... all-time Huskies leading scorer with 2,708 points (22.2); graduated as the ninth all-time NCAA Division One scorer... all-time leading shot blocker in Huskie history with 155... led Northeastern to four consecutive ECAC North Atlantic Conference titles as well as four straight trips to the NCAA Tournament... earned ECAC North Atlantic Conference Rookie of the Year honors... first ever three-time ECAC NAC Player of the Year, '85, '86, '87... the Huskies went 102-26 in his four years on Huntington Avenue, with a 72-6 conference record during that span... tri-captain in junior and senior years... had his jersey (number 35) retired in ceremonies on 1/21/89.

PERSONAL: Reggie Lewis is single... played high school ball with NBA players Reggie Williams, Tyrone Bogues, and David Wingate; that team once went 50-0 in a season... most memorable Christmas was when his mom made him open the gifts on Christmas Eve, something he had always wanted to do... considers his mom as the most influential person in his life... maintains residence year-round in the Boston area... signed on with the Boys and Girls Clubs of Boston in an effort to teach youths the road to success is not paved with guns and drugs... as a youngster, he admired George Gervin... lists football as his favorite sport outside of basketball... shoe size is 13.

TOP REGULAR SEASON PERFORMANCES

Points
42 vs. New York (4-14-91)
39 at Philadelphia (3-28-89)
35 vs. Portland (3-29-89)
34 vs. New York (4-15-90)
34 at Washington (1-12-91)
33 at Chicago (12-6-88)

Rebounds
12 at New York (1-18-91)
12 at Washington (1-12-91)
12 at Utah (3-13-91)
12 vs. Cleveland (4-14-89)
11 vs. Detroit (1-10-90)
11 vs. Detroit (1-23-91)

Assists
9 vs. Orlando (4-18-90)
9 at LA Lakers (2-18-90)
8 vs. LA Clippers (1-5-90)
7 vs. Detroit (1-23-91)

NBA RECORD

Year	Team	G	Min	FGM	FGA	Pct	FTM	FTA	Pct	Off	Def	Tot	Ast	PF-Dq	St	Bl	Pts	Avg
87-88	Bos.	49	405	90	193	.466	40	57	.702	28	35	63	26	54-0	16	15	220	4.5
88-89	Bos.	81	2657	604	1242	.486	284	361	.787	116	261	377	218	258-5	124	72	1495	18.5
89-90	Bos.	79	2522	540	1089	.496	256	317	.808	109	238	347	225	216-2	88	63	1340	17.0
90-91	Bos.	79	2878	598	1219	.491	281	340	.826	119	291	410	201	234-1	98	85	1478	18.7
TOTALS:		288	8462	1832	3743	.489	861	1075	.801	372	825	1197	670	762-8	326	235	4533	15.7

Three-Point Field Goals: 1987-88, 0-for-4 (.000); 1988-89, 3-for-22 (.136); 1989-90, 4-for-15 (.267); 1990-91, 1-for-13 (.077).
Totals: 8-for-54 (.148).

PLAYOFF RECORD

Year	Team	G	Min	FGM	FGA	Pct	FTM	FTA	Pct	Off	Def	Tot	Ast	PF-Dq	St	Bl	Pts	Avg
87-88	Bos.	12	70	13	34	.382	3	5	.600	9	7	16	4	13-0	3	2	29	2.4
88-89	Bos.	3	125	26	55	.473	9	13	.692	5	16	21	11	11-0	5	0	61	20.3
89-90	Bos.	5	200	37	62	.597	27	35	.771	9	16	25	22	14-0	7	2	101	20.2
90-91	Bos.	11	462	95	195	.487	56	68	.824	18	50	68	32	33-1	12	6	246	22.4
TOTALS:		31	857	171	346	.494	95	121	.785	41	89	130	69	71-1	27	10	437	14.1

Three-Point Field Goals: 1987-88, 0-for-1 (.000); 1988-89, 0-for-2 (.000); 1989-90, 0-for-1 (.000); 1990-91, 0-for-4 (.000).
Totals: 0-for-8 (.000).

SEASON/CAREER HIGHS

	FGM	FGA	FTM	FTA	REB	AST	ST	BL	PTS
1990-91/Regular Season	16/16	25/30	10/11	12/15	12/12	7/9	5/5	5/5	42/42
1991/Playoffs	11/11	27/27	8/8	11/11	11/11	5/9	3/3	2/2	30/30

KEVIN McHALE

Birthdate: December 19, 1957
Birthplace: Hibbing, MN
High School: Hibbing High (MN)
College: Minnesota '80
Height: 6-10
Weight: 225
NBA Experience: 11 Years

HOW ACQUIRED: Celtics first-round draft choice in 1980... 3rd pick overall.

1990-91 SEASON: Performed spectacularly throughout the season finishing among the NBA's choice in field goal percentage (8th) and blocks (8th)... received the third highest vote total in the Miller Genuine Draft NBA Sixth Man Award ballotting... was named to the All-NBA Interview Second Team... missed 14 games due to injury, team went 8-6... returned to the lineup vs. Chicago on 3/31 and played 20 minutes after suffering an aggravated left ankle before the 3/17 game vs. Philadelphia; missed the next 6 games... came back on 3/1 after missing the previous 8 games (team went 5-3) due to a sprained left ankle suffered at Seattle on 2/12... selected to the all-star game: 14 minutes, 3 rebounds, 2 assists, 1 steal, and 2 points (0-3, 0-1, 2-2)... passed Sam Jones as the club's 4th top scorer on 2/3 vs. Washington, and concluded the season with 15,793 points... 10 straight starts from 1/8-1/27: 404 minutes, 220 points (85-173, 2-4, 48-53), 91 rebounds, and 28 blocks... on 12/19 vs. Philly, his 800th regular season game, became the 54th player to score 15,000 pts... made 31 of 46 (.674) fgs in 4 games vs. Miami, had 14 blocks vs. the Heat... 1+ block in the season's first 15 games... 5+ blocks 7 times... had a string of 22 games with at least one block snapped on 4/14 vs. New York... 10+ mins 68 times... 20+ mins 63 times... 30+ mins 40 times... 40+ mins 7 times... 10+ pts 63 times... 20+ pts 30 times... 30+ pts 3 times... 10+ rebs 14 times... 14 double-doubles... **1991 Playoffs:** led Boston with 22 points in Game Three at Indiana... was scintillating in Game Six at Detroit with a career high-tying 34 points... was second to Reggie Lewis in points per game at 20.7, and led the squad with 14 blocked shots.

PROFESSIONAL CAREER: Drafted by Boston on the first-round of the 1980 draft after Golden State took Joe Barry Carroll and Utah chose Darrell Griffith... came extremely close to playing in Italy (with Trieste) before signing with the Celtics in September, 1980... named to the NBA All-Rookie Team in 1981... preserved Boston's win in Game Six of Celtics-Sixers 1981 playoff series by blocking Andrew Toney's shot and then grabbing the rebound in the final seconds... started 32 times in the 1981-82 season... named to the All-Defensive Second Team in 1983, 1989, and 1990... named to the All-Defensive First Team in 1986, 1987, and 1988... recipient of NBA's Sixth Man Award in 1984 and 1985... started 31 times in 1984-85,

including 26 consecutive starts from 2/18-4/11... scored 56 points vs. Detroit on March 3, 1985 for what was then a team record... shares team record for field goals made in a game with 22... scored 42 points in New York in game following 56 point effort; 98 points in consecutive games is a team record... played in 413 consecutive games before missing on 12/21/84... in Game Four of the 1984 NBA Finals, his famous takedown of Kurt Rambis helped propel Boston to a win... became a starter in frontcourt when Celtics dealt Cedric Maxwell to the LA Clippers on 9/6/85... suffered a sore left Achilles in the 1985-86 season, causing him to miss 14 games... Boston's leading scorer in the 1985 and 1986 NBA Finals... 30+ points in 61 regular season games... became the first player in NBA history to shoot 60% from the floor and 80% from the free throw line in one season in 1986-87... became the fourth Celtic to register 2,000 points in a season when he accomplished that in 1986-87... finished among the NBA's top ten field goal shooters in each of the last six years, including first place finishes in 1986-87 and 1987-88... began the 1987-88 season on the injured list due to right foot surgery... scored the 10,000th point of his career on 1/12/88... hit a game-tying three-point field goal with 5 seconds left in the first overtime of Game Two of the Celtics-Pistons Eastern Conference Finals (5/26/88)... became the eighth Celtic to grab 5,000 rebounds, on 2/1/89... was the only Celtic to play in all 82 games in 1989-90... scored 10+ points in 247 straight games; snapped on 11/18/89 at Detroit... had a career best free throw streak snapped at 44 on 12/13/89...in 1989-90, became the first player to finish in the top ten in fg% in the same season since Atlanta's Lou Hudson in 1969-70... starts by season: 1980-81 (1), 1981-82 (32), 1982-83 (13), 1983-84 (10), 1984-85 (31), 1985-86 (62), 1986-87 (77), 1987-88 (63), 1988-89 (74), 1989-90 (25), 1990-91 (10).

COLLEGE CAREER: First Team All-Big Ten selection by AP and UPI in 1979-80... graduated as Minnesota's second leading scorer (1,704 points) and rebounder (950)... team MVP in 1980... MVP of the Pillsbury Classic three times... MVP of the Aloha Classic in 1980... starter on the Gold Medal-winning Pan American Team in the summer of 1979... started on the Gold Medal-winning World University Games Team in 1979... named to the All-Big Ten Team for the decade of the 1970's.

PERSONAL: Kevin Edward McHale and his wife Lynn have four children, Kristyn (5/9/83), Michael (2/23/85), Joseph (12/10/86), and Alexandra (10/27/89)... favorite recreational sports are golfing and fishing; likes to play backgammon... a big-time hockey fan, he is an ardent supporter of the Boston Bruins... returns to Minnesota in the summer... enjoys the music of Bruce Springsteen and Bob Dylan, who is also from Hibbing, MN... lists his dad as his most instrumental person... appeared as himself on the television show "Cheers", which originally aired in September, 1990... as a youngster, his favorite athlete was Jack Nicklaus ... shoe size is 15 and a half.

TOP REGULAR SEASON PERFORMANCES

Points
56 vs. Detroit (3-3-85)
42 at New York (3-5-85)
38 vs. Detroit (3-1-87)
38 vs. Cleveland (1-16-87)

seven times

Rebounds
18 at LA Clippers (12-30-85)
18 at Detroit (1-16-89)
17 at Cleveland (1-23-88)
17 vs. Indiana (3-11-88)

Assists
10 vs. Dallas (4-3-88)
9 vs. Philadelphia (3-25-88)
8 at New Jersey (4-9-86)

7

NBA RECORD

Year	Team	G	Min	FGM	FGA	Pct	FTM	FTA	Pct	Off	Def	Tot	Ast	PF-Dq	St	Bl	Pts	Avg
80-81	Bos.	82	1645	355	666	.533	108	159	.679	155	204	359	55	260-3	27	151	818	10.0
81-82	Bos.	82	2332	465	875	.531	187	248	.754	191	365	556	91	264-1	30	185	1117	13.6
82-83	Bos.	82	2345	483	893	.541	193	269	.717	215	338	553	104	241-3	34	192	1159	14.1
83-84	Bos.	82	2577	587	1055	.556	336	439	.765	208	402	610	104	243-5	23	126	1511	18.4
84-85	Bos.	79	2653	605	1062	.570	355	467	.760	229	483	712	141	234-3	28	120	1565	19.8
85-86	Bos.	68	2397	561	978	.574	326	420	.776	171	380	551	181	192-2	29	134	1448	21.3
86-87	Bos.	77	3060	790	1307	.604	428	512	.836	247	516	763	198	240-1	38	172	2008	26.1
87-88	Bos.	64	2390	550	911	.604	346	434	.797	159	377	536	171	179-1	27	92	1446	22.6
88-89	Bos.	78	2876	661	1211	.546	436	533	.818	223	414	637	172	223-2	26	97	1758	22.5
89-90	Bos.	82	2722	648	1181	.549	393	440	.893	201	476	677	172	250-3	30	157	1712	20.9
90-91	Bos.	68	2067	504	912	.553	228	275	.829	145	335	480	126	194-2	25	146	1251	18.4
TOTALS:		844	27046	6209	11051	.562	3336	4196	.795	2144	4290	6434	1515	2520-26	317	1572	15793	18.7

Three-Point Field Goals: 1980-81, 0-for-2 (.000); 1982-83, 0-for-1 (.000); 1983-84, 1-for-3 (.333); 1984-85, 0-for-6 (.000); 1986-87, 0-for-4 (.000); 1988-89, 0-for-4 (.000); 1989-90, 23-for-69 (.333); 1990-91, 15-for-37 (.405).
Totals: 39-for-126 (.310).

PLAYOFF RECORD

Year	Team	G	Min	FGM	FGA	Pct	FTM	FTA	Pct	Off	Def	Tot	Ast	PF-Dq	St	Bl	Pts	Avg
80-81	Bos.	17	296	61	113	.540	23	36	.639	29	30	59	14	51-1	4	25	145	8.5
81-82	Bos.	12	344	77	134	.575	40	53	.755	41	44	85	11	44-0	5	27	194	16.2
82-83	Bos.	7	177	34	62	.548	10	18	.556	15	27	42	5	16-0	3	7	78	11.1
83-84	Bos.	23	702	123	244	.504	94	121	.777	62	81	143	27	75-1	3	35	340	14.8
84-85	Bos.	21	837	172	303	.568	121	150	.807	74	134	208	32	73-3	13	46	465	22.1
85-86	Bos.	18	715	168	290	.579	112	141	.794	51	104	155	48	64-0	8	43	448	24.9
86-87	Bos.	21	827	174	298	.584	96	126	.762	66	128	194	39	71-2	7	30	444	21.1
87-88	Bos.	17	716	158	262	.603	115	137	.839	55	81	136	40	65-1	7	30	432	25.4
88-89	Bos.	3	115	20	41	.448	17	23	.739	7	17	24	9	13-0	1	2	57	19.0
89-90	Bos.	5	192	42	69	.609	25	29	.862	8	31	39	13	17-0	2	10	110	22.0
90-91	Bos.	11	376	78	148	.527	66	80	.825	18	54	72	20	42-0	5	14	228	20.7
TOTALS:		155	5297	1107	1964	.564	719	914	.787	426	731	1157	258	531-8	58	269	2941	19.0

Three-Point Field Goals: 1982-83, 0-for-1 (.000); 1983-84, 0-for-3 (.000); 1985-86, 0-for-1 (.000); 1987-88, 1-for-1 (1.000); 1989-90, 1-for-3 (.333); 1990-91, 6-for-11 (.545). Totals: 8-for-20 (.400).

ALL STAR RECORD

Year	Team	Min	FGM	FGA	Pct	FTM	FTA	Pct	Off	Def	Tot	Ast	PF-Dq	St	Bl	Pts	Avg
1984	Bos.	11	3	7	.429	4	6	.667	2	3	5	0	1-0	0	0	10	10.0
1986	Bos.	20	3	38	.375	2	2	1.000	3	7	10	2	4-0	0	4	8	8.0
1987	Bos.	30	7	11	.636	2	2	1.000	4	3	7	2	5-0	0	4	16	16.0
1988	Bos.	14	0	1	.000	2	2	1.000	0	1	1	1	2-0	0	2	2	2.0
1989	Bos.	16	5	7	.714	0	0	.000	`1	2	3	0	3-0	0	2	10	10.0
1990	Bos.	20	6	11	.545	0	0	.000	2	6	8	1	4-0	0	0	13	13.0
1991	Bos.	14	0	3	.000	2	2	1.000	1	2	3	2	2-0	1	0	2	2.0
TOTALS:		125	24	48	.500	12	14	.857	13	24	37	8	21-0	1	12	61	8.7

Three-Point Field Goals: 1990, 1-for-1 (1.000); 1991, 0-for-1 (.000). Totals: 1-for-2 (.500).

SEASON/CAREER HIGHS

	FGM	FGA	FTM	FTA	REB	AST	ST	BL	PTS
1990-91/Regular Season	13/22	24/30	9/15	10/19	15/18	7/10	2/3	5/9	32/56
1991/Playoffs	13/15	21/25	11/14	14/16	10/17	6/7	2/3	4/6	34/34

ROBERT PARISH

Birthdate: August 30, 1953
Birthplace: Shreveport, LA
High School: Woodlawn (Shreveport, LA)
College: Centenary '76
Height: 7-1/2
Weight: 230
Position: Center
Years Pro: 14 Years

How Acquired: Traded by Golden State with a 1980 first-round draft choice for two 1980 first-round draft choices on June 9, 1980.

1989-90 Season: Named to the Eastern Conference All-Star reserves; had 14 pts (7-11, 0-1) and 4 rebs in 21 mins, and tied for second place in the MVP voting... 31 points (12-14, 7-10) with 17 rebs at the Cavs on 11/11...10-12 fgs at Hawks on 11/25... in two games vs. the Lakers: 79 mins, 43 pts (19-28, 5-9), 24 rebs... made all 7 fgs on 12/5 at Hornets... scored 38 pts (tied for second best of career) on 12/8 vs. Denver... 29 pts (12-15 fgs) at the Bullets on 1/6... had three key rebs in last minute vs. Knicks, on 1/31...10+ mins 78 times... 20+ mins 74 times... 30+ mins 44 times... 40+ mins 5 times...10+ rebs 44 times... 10+ pts 65 times... 20+ pts 17 times... 30+ pts 3 times... 43 double-doubles... surpassed the 18,000 point mark on 3/7... made 21 straight fts from 2/25-3/21... started 78 times, including the first 60 games and the regular season's final 18... suffered a hyperextended right knee vs. Philly on 3/11, causing him to miss the next three games... returned to action on 3/18... shot 49-70 (.700) from the field in the last six games of March... his fg% was the second highest of his career... started all five playoff games, averaging 15.8 ppg; made 17 of 18 fts, and led Boston with 50 rebounds... received a pair of votes to the All-NBA team.

Professional Career: Drafted by Golden State on the first-round of the 1976 draft, the 8th pick overall... had an incredible game on 3/30/79 against the Knicks when he scored 30 points and grabbed 32 rebounds... traded to Boston along with a pick that turned out to be Kevin McHale; in return, Boston traded two number one picks to the Warriors, which selected Joe Barry Carroll and Rickey Brown... became Boston's force in the middle when Dave Cowens suddenly retired... runner-up to Larry Bird in the 1982 All-Star MVP balloting... shares the team record with 9 blocks on 3/17/82... named to the All-NBA Second Team in 1982... scored the 10,000th point of his career on 2/26/84 in Phoenix... had two key steals in the waning moments of overtime in Game Two of the 1984 Finals... represented the Celtics in the All-Star Game eight times... played in 99 of 100 games in the 1985-86 season... is the only Celtic to grab 25+ rebounds in a game (accomplished twice) since the 1977-78 season... registered his lone triple-double on 3/29/87 vs. the Sixers... missed Game Six of the 1987 series at Milwaukee, snapping a streak of 116 straight playoff appearances... finished second to teammate Kevin McHale in field goal accuracy during the 1987-88 season; in fact, he has been in the NBA's top ten in each of the past six years... grabbed his 10,000th rebound on 2/22/89... named to the All-NBA Third Team in 1989.

College Career: Named to The Sporting News All-America First Team in 1976... a Gold Medalist in the 1975 World University Games, a team coached by Dave Gavitt... played four years at Centenary... once had 50 points in a game against So. Miss... grabbed 33 rebounds in a game... averaged 21.6 points in 108 career games... averaged 23.0 points as a freshman, and 24.8 as a senior... made 56.4% of his fgs.

Personal: Robert L. Parish is single... relaxes to jazz music... other enjoyments include judo, backgammon and horror films... nicknamed "Chief" by Cedric Maxwell, after a character in "One Flew Over the Cuckoo's Nest"... resides in the Boston area year-round... went to the same high school as former NFL star Terry Bradshaw... holds a basketball camp at New Hampshire College during the summer... most memorable Christmas moment: the spirit of giving and receiving with his family as a youngster... lists Bill Russell, Wilt Chamberlain, and Clifford Ray as his favorite athletes... names his dad as his most influential person... shoe size is 16.

Career Highs: 32 rebounds vs. New York (3-30-79).

TOP REGULAR SEASON PERFORMANCES (WITH CELTICS)

Points
40 at San Antonio (2-17-81)
38 vs. Houston (3-17-85)
38 vs. Denver (12-8-89)
37 at Philadelphia (3-21-82)

Rebounds
25 vs. Sacramento (1-9-87)
25 at Washington (3-8-86)
24 at Charlotte (2-1-89)
23 two times

Assists
10 vs. Philadelphia (3-29-87)
9 at Detroit (11-15-86)
7 at Chicago (1-21-83)
7 vs. Seattle (2-5-89)

NBA RECORD

Year	Team	G	Min	FGM	FGA	Pct	FTM	FTA	Pct	Off	Def	Tot	Ast	PF-Dq	St	Bl	Pts	Avg
76-77	G.S.	77	1384	288	573	.503	121	171	.708	201	342	543	74	224-7	55	94	697	9.1
77-78	G.S.	82	1969	430	911	.472	165	264	.625	211	469	680	95	291-10	79	123	1025	12.5
78-79	G.S.	76	2411	554	1110	.499	196	281	.698	265	651	916	115	303-10	100	217	1304	17.2
79-80	G.S.	72	2119	510	1006	.507	203	284	.715	247	536	783	122	248-6	58	115	1223	17.0
80-81	Bos.	82	2298	635	1166	.545	282	397	.710	245	532	777	144	310-9	81	214	1552	18.9
81-82	Bos.	80	2534	669	1235	.542	252	355	.710	288-	578	866	140	267-5	68	192	1590	19.9
82-83	Bos.	78	2459	619	1125	.550	271	388	.698	260	567	827	141	222-4	79	148	1509	19.3
83-84	Bos.	80	2867	623	1140	.546	274	368	.745	243	614	857	139	266-7	55	116	1520	19.0
84-85	Bos.	79	2850	551	1016	.542	292	393	.743	263	577	840	125	223-2	56	101	1394	17.6
85-86	Bos.	81	2567	530	966	.549	245	335	.731	246	524	770	145	215-3	65	116	1305	16.1
86-87	Bos.	80	2995	588	1057	.556	227	309	.735	254	597	851	173	266-5	64	144	1403	17.5
87-88	Bos.	74	2312	442	750	.589	177	241	.734	173	455	628	115	198-5	55	84	1061	14.3
88-89	Bos.	80	2840	596	1045	.570	294	409	.719	342	654	996	175	209-2	79	116	1486	18.6
89-90	Bos.	79	2396	505	871	.580	233	312	.747	259	537	796	103	189-2	38	69	1243	15.7
90-91	Bos.	81	2441	485	811	.598	237	309	.767	271	585	856	66	197-1	66	103	1207	14.9
TOTALS:		1181	36442	8025	14782	.543	3469	4816	.720	3768	8218	11986	1872	3628-78	998	1952	19519	16.5

Three-Point Field Goals: 1979-80, 0-for-1 (.000); 1980-81, 0-for-1 (.000); 1982-83, 0-for-1 (.000); 1986-87, 0-for-1 (.000); 1987-88, 0-for-1 (.000); 1990-91, 0-for-1 (.000). Totals: 0-for-6 (.000).

PLAYOFF RECORD

Year	Team	G	Min	FGM	FGA	Pct	FTM	FTA	Pct	Off	Def	Tot	Ast	PF-Dq	St	Bl	Pts	Avg
76-77	G.S.	10	239	52	108	.481	17	26	.654	43	60	103	11	42-1	7	11	121	12.1
80-81	Bos.	17	492	108	219	.493	39	58	.672	50	96	146	19	74-2	21	39	255	15.0
81-82	Bos.	12	426	102	209	.488	51	75	.680	43	92	135	18	47-1	5	48	255	21.3
82-83	Bos.	7	249	43	89	.483	17	20	.850	21	53	74	9	18-0	5	9	103	14.7
83-84	Bos.	23	869	139	291	.478	64	99	.646	76	172	248	27	100-6	23	41	342	14.9
84-85	Bos.	21	803	136	276	.493	87	111	.784	57	162	219	31	68-0	21	34	359	17.1
85-86	Bos.	18	591	106	225	.471	58	89	.652	52	106	158	25	47-1	9	30	270	15.0
86-87	Bos.	21	734	149	263	.567	79	103	.767	59	139	198	28	79-4	18	35	377	18.0
87-88	Bos.	17	626	100	188	.532	50	61	.820	51	117	168	21	42-0	11	19	250	14.7
88-89	Bos.	3	112	20	44	.455	7	9	.778	6	20	26	6	5-0	4	2	47	15.7
89-90	Bos.	5	170	31	54	.574	17	18	.944	23	27	50	13	21-0	5	7	79	15.8
90-91	Bos.	10	296	58	97	.598	42	61	.689	33	59	92	6	34-1	8	7	158	15.8
TOTALS:		164	5607	1044	2063	.506	528	730	.723	514	1103	1617	214	577-16	137	282	2616	16.0

Three-Point Field Goals: 1986-87, 0-for-1 (.000).

ALL STAR GAME RECORD

Year	Team	Min	FGM	FGA	Pct	FTM	FTA	Pct	Off	Def	Tot	Ast	PF-Dq	St	Bl	Pts	Avg
1981	Bos.	25	5	18	.278	6	6	1.000	6	4	10	2	3-0	0	2	16	16.0
1982	Bos.	20	9	12	.750	3	4	.750	0	7	7	1	2-0	0	2	21	21.0
1983	Bos.	18	5	6	.833	3	4	.750	0	3	3	0	2-0	1	1	13	13.0
1984	Bos.	28	5	11	.455	2	4	.500	4	11	15	2	1-0	3	0	12	12.0
1985	Bos.	10	2	5	.400	0	0	.000	3	3	6	1	0-0	0	0	4	4.0
1986	Bos.	7	0	0	.000	0	2	.000	0	1	1	0	0-0	0	1	0	0.0
1987	Bos.	8	2	3	.667	0	0	.000	0	3	3	0	1-0	0	1	4	4.0
1990	Bos.	21	7	11	.636	0	1	.000	2	2	4	2	4-0	0	1	14	14.0
1991	Bos.	5	1	2	.500	0	0	.000	1	3	4	0	2-0	0	0	2	2.0
TOTALS:		142	36	68	.529	14	21	.667	16	37	53	8	15-0	4	8	86	9.6

Three-Point Field Goals: None attempted.

SEASON/CAREER HIGHS

	FGM	FGA	FTM	FTA	REB	AST	ST	BL	PTS
1990-91/Regular Season	13/16	18/31	9/13	11/18	20/32	4/10	3/6	5/9	29/40
1991/Playoffs	10/14	14/25	7/11	10/15	13/19	3/6	3/5	2/7	21/33

ED PINCKNEY

Birthdate: March 27, 1963
Birthplace: Bronx, NY
High School: Adlai Stevenson High (NY)
College: Villanova '85
Height: 6-9
Weight: 215
NBA Experience: 6 Years

HOW ACQUIRED: Traded by Sacramento with Joe Kleine to Boston for Danny Ainge and Brad Lohaus on February 23, 1989.

1990-91 SEASON: Completed his second full season in a Celtics uniform, and his play improved as the season progressed... established a career high in free throw percentage... made 14 straight field goals from 3/28-4/4, and 23 of 30 (.767) over 8 games from 3/22-4/11... tied a career best 17 rebounds at Orlando on 4/6... had a pair of 15 rebound outings, 1/28 at Minnesota and 4/4 vs. New Jersey... great outing vs. Cleveland on 3/29, as he tallied 35 minutes, 19 points (7-7, 5-7), and 14 rebounds... made 26 straight free throws before missing on 3/29... 4 blocks at Golden State on 2/14... last 4 games of 1990: 63 minutes, 42 points (16-24, 10-11) and 20 rebounds... vs. Indiana on 11/26: tabulated 14 points and 9 rebounds in just 19 minutes... had 29 rebounds in 2 starts vs. Orlando... team went 9-7 in his starts (11/2, 11/6-11/10, 1/28-2/3, 2/7, 4/6-4/19); 337 mins, 96 pts (32-76, 32-35), 113 rebs... 16-23 (.696) fgs at Pacific Division teams... 10+ mins 57 times... 20+ mins 22 times... 30+ mins 4 times... 10+ pts 10 times... 10+ rebs 8 times... 3 double-doubles... DNP-CD 12 times (last was 12/19)... **1991 Playoffs:** for the second straight season he posted a dazzling field goal percentage; shot .762 (16-21) from the floor in 11 outings... was a key figure in Boston's incredible comeback run in Game Six at Detroit, as he was one of five players, who fought back from an 80-65 deficit without substitution until the overtime's last 12 seconds.

PROFESSIONAL CAREER: Drafted by Phoenix on the first-round of the 1985 draft, the 10th pick overall... played his first two professional seasons with the Suns... traded to the Kings on June 21, 1987, along with a 1988 second-round draft choice in exchange for Eddie Johnson... had seven starts in the 1987-88 season... led the Kings in field goal percentage in 1987-88 (.522)... played 54 games with the Kings in 1988-89, including 24 starts... led Sacramento by shooting 50.2% in 1988-89 before the trade to Boston... started nine times in his initial season with Boston... started 50 times in 1989-90... had 16 points in 14 minutes in Game Two of the 1990 playoff opener against New York.

COLLEGE CAREER: Member of the 1985 NCAA Champions... chosen MVP of the NCAA Division One Tournament in 1985... honorable mention All-America as a sophomore, junior, and senior... led the Wildcats in blocks, rebounds, and fg% all four years... 1983 Gold Medal-winner in the Pan American Games... graduated as Villanova's fifth best scorer (1,865), fourth best rebounder (1,107), and top field goal shooter (.604)... remarkably, his lowest fg% was .568 as a sophomore.

PERSONAL: Edward Lewis Pinckney and his wife Rose have two children, Shea (11/5/84) and Spence (8/22/88)... nicknamed "E-Z Ed" ... has seven sisters... involved in People Reaching Out (PRO), a family counseling center specializing in prevention and intervention of drug and alcohol abuse... favorite television show is "The Fugitive"... favorite NBA city (outside Boston) is New York... likes playing in Madison Square Garden... names Julius Erving as the best player he has ever seen... favorite pregame meal is pasta... most influential person is his dad... graduated with a degree in Communications... most memorable Christmas was junior year in college, spending it at Disney World during a basketball tournament in Orlando... likes playing softball and handball... lives in New Jersey during the summer... shoe size is 13.

CAREER HIGHS: 27 points vs. Seattle (3-26-86)
17 rebounds at Chicago (11-8-86)
6 assists vs. Houston (4-1-87)

TOP REGULAR SEASON PERFORMANCES

Points
22 vs. San Antonio (3-20-89)
22 vs. Portland (3-29-89)
19 vs. New York (3-24-89)
19 vs. Chicago (4-20-89)
19 vs. Orlando (1-30-91)
19 vs. Cleveland (3-29-91)

Rebounds
17 at Orlando (4-6-91)
15 at Minnesota (1-28-91)
14 vs. Cleveland (3-29-91)
12 vs. Orlando (1-30-91)
12 at Detroit (4-16-91)

Assists
6 at Indiana (3-16-89)
5 at Detroit (3-17-89)
5 at Orlando (1-17-90)
5 vs. Chicago (11-9-91)

NBA RECORD

Year	Team	G	Min	FGM	FGA	Pct	FTM	FTA	Pct	Off	Def	Tot	Ast	PF-Dq	St	Bl	Pts	Avg
85-86	Pho.	80	1602	255	457	.558	171	254	.673	95	213	308	90	190-3	71	37	681	8.5
86-87	Pho.	80	2250	290	497	.584	257	348	.739	179	401	580	116	196-1	86	54	837	10.5
87-88	Sac.	79	1177	179	343	.522	133	178	.747	94	136	230	66	118-0	39	32	491	6.2
88-89	Sac/Bos	80	2012	319	622	.513	280	350	.800	166	283	449	118	202-2	83	66	918	11.5
89-90	Bos.	77	1082	135	249	.542	92	119	.773	93	132	225	68	126-1	34	42	362	4.7
90-91	Bos.	70	1165	131	243	.539	104	116	.897	155	186	341	45	147-0	61	43	366	5.2
TOTALS:		466	9288	1309	2411	.543	1037	1365	.760	782	1351	2133	503	979-7	374	274	3655	7.8

Three-Point Field Goals: 1985-86, 0-for-2 (.000); 1986-87, 0-for-2 (.000); 1987-88, 0-for-2 (.000); 1988-89, 0-for-6 (.000);1988-89, 0-for-1 (.000); 1989-90, 0-for-1 (.000). Totals:0-for-14 (.000).

PLAYOFF RECORD

Year	Team	G	Min	FGM	FGA	Pct	FTM	FTA	Pct	Off	Def	Tot	Ast	PF-Dq	St	Bl	Pts	Avg
88-89	Bos.	3	112	20	44	.455	7	9	.778	6	20	26	6	5-0	4	2	47	15.7
89-90	Bos.	4	25	6	7	.857	7	9	.778	2	4	6	0	3-0	0	0	19	4.8
90-91	Bos.	11	170	16	21	.762	17	21	.810	23	17	40	2	17-0	6	2	49	4.5
TOTALS:		18	240	25	40	.625	26	32	.813	27	24	51	3	27-0	7	3	76	4.2

Three-Point Field Goals: None attempted.

SEASON/CAREER HIGHS

	FGM	FGA	FTM	FTA	REB	AST	ST	BL	PTS
1990-91/Regular Season	7/10	13/16	7/12	8/15	17/17	5/6	3/6	4/4	19/27
1991/Playoffs	6/6	6/6	8/8	8/8	9/9	1/1	2/2	1/1	13/16

BRIAN SHAW

Birthdate: March 22, 1966
Birthplace: Oakland, CA
High School: Bishop O'Dowd High (CA)
College: Cal-Santa Barbara '88
Height: 6-6
Weight: 190
NBA Experience: 2 Years

HOW ACQUIRED: Celtics first-round draft choice in 1988... 24th pick overall.

1990-91 SEASON: In his return to the NBA, after a one-year stint in Italy, Boston's top draft choice of 1988 made an immediate impact by hitting a game-winner buzzer-beater in Chicago on 11/6... made 31 of 32 fts from 11/10-11/24... made 25 of 39 (.641) fgs in Boston's 3-game swing of Texas from 12/7-12/10... 3 games from 1/27-1/30: he scored 69 points (31-52, 7-8)... suffered a sprained right ankle after 3 minutes vs. Portland on 3/3; did not play in the next 3 games, the only games he failed to start... dished out 15 assists vs. Chicago on 3/31; had a career high 17 assists vs. Miami on 4/12... tallied 47 points in 2 games vs. Orlando... 0 to's/ 30+ mins 5 times... 10+ mins 78 times... 20+ mins 77 times... 30+ mins 65 times... 40+ mins 21 times... 10+ pts 54 times... 20+ pts 18 times... 10+ rebs 2 times... 10+ asts 17 times... 13 double-doubles...
1991 Playoffs: was one of three Celtics to perform in all 11 games... had a great outing in Game Three at Detroit with 19 points, 8 rebounds, and 5 assists in 30 minutes.

PROFESSIONAL CAREER: Drafted by Boston on the first-round of the 1988 draft, the 24th pick overall... the only Celtic to play in every game in 1988-89... started the last 45 regular season games, and a total of 54 during his rookie season... numbers as a starter: 54 games, 1769 mins, 227-517 (.439) fgs, 0-6 (.000) 3-ptrs, 78-94 (.830) fts, 295 rebs (5.5), 349 assts (6.5), 532 pts (9.9) in 1988-89... 10+ mins 81 times... 20+ mins 68 times... 30+ mins 36 times... 40+ mins 12 times... 10+ rebs 9 times... 10+ assts 12 times... 15 double-doubles... 10+ pts 31 times... 20+ pts twice... 30+ pts once... had the most starts by a Celtics' rookie since Larry Bird in 1979-80, and became the first Celtics' rookie to play in every game since Kevin McHale in 1980-81... was the only Celtics' player to register three 40+ minute outputs in the 1989 playoffs... chosen to the NBA All-Rookie Second Team (was the sixth highest point getter among NBA rookies)... signed with Il Messaggero Roma of the A-1 Italian League on August 10, 1989... scored a game high 46 points in a season-ending playoff loss to Scavolini Pesaro... original announcement of his return to the Celtics was made on February 27, 1990... after a lengthy court battle, he re-signed with Boston on September 17, 1990.

COLLEGE CAREER: Named the Pacific Coast Athletic Association Player of the Year after his senior season... became the first point guard in PCAA history to lead the conference in rebounding with 9.1 rpg... originally attended St. Mary's (CA) playing in 41 games over two years... sat out 1985-86 as a redshirt... transferred to UCSB and was Second Team All-PCAA in 1986-87... emerged as one of the West Coast's top players in senior season, posting averages of 13.3 ppg, 8.8 rpg and 6.1 apg... became Santa Barbara's all-time leader in assists (375) in 59 games over two seasons... connected on 44 of 116 three-pointers for a .379 accuracy mark in two years at UCSB... helped lead Santa Barbara to an NCAA Tournament appearance.

PERSONAL: Brian K. Shaw is single... lists fishing, particularly in Alaska, and playing cards as his hobbies... enjoys rap music... favorite recreational sports are basketball, football, and baseball... names Magic Johnson as the greatest player he's seen... preferred pregame meal is pasta, while his favorite food is gumbo... is a spokesman for the Big Brother Association... as a youngster, he rooted for the Los Angeles Lakers... lists his parents as his childhood heroes... lists his dad as his most influential person... returns to California in the summer... shoe size is 14.

TOP REGULAR SEASON PERFORMANCES

Points	Rebounds	Assists
31 at Phoenix (2-17-89)	15 at Atlanta (4-13-89)	17 vs. Miami (4-12-91)
26 at Houston (12-10-90)	14 at Philadelphia (3-28-89)	15 vs. Chicago (3-31-91)
26 vs. Indiana(12-26-90)	12 at Charlotte (4-17-89)	14 vs. Utah (11-16-90)
26 vs. Orlando (1-30-91)	12 at Houston (12-10-91)	13 four times
26 vs. NJ @ Htfd (2-22-91)	11 four times	

NBA RECORD

Year	Team	G	Min	FGM	FGA	Pct	FTM	FTA	Pct	Off	Def	Tot	Ast	PF-Dq	St	Bl	Pts	Avg
88-89	Bos.	82	2301	297	686	.433	109	132	.826	119	257	376	472	211-1	78	27	703	8.6
89-90	Roma	30	1144	244	418	.584	111	139	.799	71	203	274	69	NA-NA	80	18	749	25.0
90-91	Bos	79	2772	442	942	.469	204	249	.819	104	266	370	602	206-1	105	34	1091	13.8
TOTALS:		161	5073	739	1628	.454	313	381	.822	223	523	746	1074	417-2	183	61	1794	11.1

Three-Point Field Goals: 1988-89, 0-for-13 (.000); 1989-90, 50-for-140 (.357); 1990-91, 3-for-27 (.111).
Totals: 3-for-40 (.075).

PLAYOFF RECORD

Year	Team	G	Min	FGM	FGA	Pct	FTM	FTA	Pct	Off	Def	Tot	Ast	PF-Dq	St	Bl	Pts	Avg
88-89	Bos.	3	124	22	43	.512	7	9	.778	2	15	17	19	11-0	3	0	51	17.0
89-90	Roma	6	228	39	68	.574	37	44	.841	13	43	56	5	19-0	9	6	151	25.2
90-91	Bos.	11	316	47	100	.470	26	30	.867	8	30	38	51	34-0	10	1	121	11.0
TOTALS:		14	440	69	143	.483	33	39	.846	10	45	55	70	45-0	13	1	172	12.3

Three-Point Field Goals: 1988-89, 0-for-1 (.000); 1989-90, 12-for-31 (.387); 1990-91, 1-for-3 (,333).
Totals: 1-for-4 (.250).

NOTE: The Italian League compiles two-point field goals and three-point field goals separately, unlike the NBA.

SEASON/CAREER HIGHS

	FGM	FGA	FTM	FTA	REB	AST	ST	BL	PTS
1990-91/Regular Season	11/14	24/24	9/9	11/11	12/15	17/17	5/7	3/3	26/31
1991/Playoffs	9/9	21/21	7/7	8/8	8/8	9/9	3/3	1/1	22/22

MICHAEL SMITH

Birthdate: May 19, 1965
Birthplace: Rochester, NY
High School: Los Altos High (Hacienda Heights, CA)
College: Brigham Young '89
Height: 6-10
Weight: 225
NBA Experience: 2 Years

HOW ACQUIRED: Celtics first-round draft choice in 1989... 13th pick overall.

1990-91 SEASON: Boston's top draft choice of 1989 started 2 of the team's first 6 games; totalled 3 (team was 2-1) starts (11/3, 11/13, 2/22) and amassed 20 minutes, 8 points (2-7, 4-4), 3 rebounds and 1 assist... he put up impressive figures in some reserve roles, including 13 points (6-8, 1-1, 0-0) in 15 minutes at Chicago on 2/26, 15 points (6-8, 1-1, 2-2) in 16 minutes at Denver on 2/17, and 23 points (11-16, 1-1, 0-0) and 6 rebounds in 18 minutes vs. Orlando on 1/30... had 4 assists in just 7 minutes vs. Seattle on 12/3... in 3 appearances from 12/3-12/15, he collected 22 points (10-16, 2-2) and 6 assists in 31 minutes... 10+ mins 19 times... 20+ mins once... 10+ pts 7 times... 20+ pts once... DNP-CD 35 times... **1991 Playoffs:** totalled six minutes in a pair of games, Games Three and Six at Detroit.

PROFESSIONAL CAREER: Began his rookie season (1989-90) on the injured list with a lower back injury and shin splints... activated on 11/17, and saw his first action that night vs. Minnesota... tallied 16 points and 8 assists in 24 minutes vs. Kings on 2/4/90... free throw breakdown by calendar year as a rookie 1989, 1-for-4, 1990, 52-for-60; began the month of February at .400 (2-for-5)... played in 40 straight games

from 1/12-4/4... DNP-CD 9 times... 10+ mins 24 times... 20+ mins 11 times... 30+ mins 5 times... 10+ pts 13 times... 20+ pts 2 times... 10+ rebs once... one double-double... started 7 straight games from 2/23 thru 3/9; his numbers: 194 mins, 102 pts (44-88, 1-11, 13-16), 27 rebs, and 15 assts.

COLLEGE CAREER: Three-time All-WAC First Team selection, averaging 19.0 points over four years... finished as BYU's second all-time leading scorer (2,319 points) behind Danny Ainge... connected on 116-for-270 (.430) three-point attempts in his career and helped lead the Cougars to three consecutive NCAA Tournament appearances... broke conference record for field goals made (previous record was 428 by Devin Durrant)... his career free throw percentage (.878) is the best in conference history... Division One ft% leader in 1988-89, making 160 of 173 shots (.925)... missed the 1984-85 and 1985-86 basketball seasons while serving on a Mormon mission in Argentina.

PERSONAL: Michael John Smith and his wife Michelle have two children, a daughter Kenya Michal (11/9/89), and a son Kennon McKay (2/28/91); couple married on October 8, 1988... majored in Spanish, and graduated with an impressive grade point average... most influential person is his oldest brother Clark Smith... lists John Havlicek, Larry Bird, Magic Johnson, Michael Jordan and Julius Erving as the greatest basketball players... a huge fan of pro beach volleyball, he played that sport and football in high school, and was the recipient of many awards in both... favorite pregame meal is pasta and wheat bread... extremely intelligent and personable... would like to go into broadcasting or real estate after his playing days are over... lists Jesus Christ as the person he'd most like to meet... returns to California during the summer... shoe size is 14.

TOP REGULAR SEASON PERFORMANCES

Points	Rebounds	Assists
24 at Denver (2-25-90)	10 at Miami (3-2-90)	8 vs. Sacramento (2-4-90)
23 vs. Orlando (1-30-91)	6 at Philadelphia (4-22-90)	6 vs. Orlando (4-18-90)
21 vs. Dallas (2-28-90)	6 vs. Orlando (1-30-91)	5 at Orlando (3-16-90)
17 vs. Orlando (4-18-90)	5 four times	4 four times
17 at Orlando (3-16-90))		

NBA RECORD

Year	Team	G	Min	FGM	FGA	Pct.	FTM	FTA	Pct.	Off	Def	Tot	Ast	PF-Dq	St	Bl	Pts	Avg
89-90	Bos.	65	620	136	286	.476	53	64	.828	40	60	100	79	51-0	9	1	327	5.0
90-91	Bos.	47	389	95	200	.475	22	27	.815	21	35	56	43	27-0	6	2	218	4.6
TOTALS:		112	1009	231	486	.475	75	91	.824	61	95	156	122	78-0	15	3	545	4.9

Three-Point Field Goals: 1989-90, 2-for-28 (.071); 1990-91, 6-for-24 (.250).
Totals: 8-for-52 (.154).

PLAYOFF RECORD

Year	Team	G	Min	FGM	FGA	Pct.	FTM	FTA	Pct.	Off	Def	Tot	Ast	PF-Dq	St	Bl	Pts	Avg
89-90	Bos.	4	16	5	8	.625	7	7	1.000	0	0	0	0	1-0	1	0	17	4.3
90-91	Bos.	2	6	1	2	.500	0	0	.000	0	0	0	1	2-0	0	0	2	1.0
TOTALS:		6	22	6	10	.600	7	7	1.000	0	0	0	1	3-0	1	0	19	3.2

Three-Point Field Goals: 1989-90, 0-for-2 (.000); 1990-91, 0-for-1 (.000).
Totals: 0-for-2 (.000).

SEASON/CAREER HIGHS

	FGM	FGA	FTM	FTA	REB	AST	ST	BL	PTS
1990-91/Regular Season	11/11	16/18	4/5	4/6	6/10	4/8	2/2	2/2	23/24
1991/Playoffs	1/4	2/5	0/4	0/4	0/0	1/1	0/1	0/0	2/9

STOJKO VRANKOVIC

Birthdate: January 22, 1964
Birthplace: Drnis, Yugoslavia
High School: N/A
College: None
Height: 7-2
Weight: 260
NBA: Experience1 Year

HOW ACQUIRED: Signed as a free agent on October 1, 1990.

1990-91 SEASON: The Celtics' Yugoslavian rookie became a fan favorite with the Boston Garden faithful... averaged a block for every five minutes he played, gaining a reputation as a forceful presence in the middle despite low minute totals; blocked shots in 16 of 30 games, including multiple blocks 9 times... appeared in 11 minutes vs. Orlando on 1/30, scored 4 points with 4 boards... with Robert Parish hurt, he saw extended duty on 1/21 at Detroit accumulating 15 minutes, 7 rebounds, 5 points, and 3 blocks... played in 7 straight games from 12/20-1/6... 10+ mins 3 times... DNP-CD 51 times... **1991 Playoffs:** played in one game, and registered four minutes.

CAREER: A member of the 1988 Yugoslavian Olympic Team, he has also been a member of the Yugoslavian National Team since 1985... would have been a definite first round 1988 draft pick... signed his first Celtics' contract on 4/29/88... due to international commitments, he was unavailable to the Celtics for the 1988-89 and 1989-90 seasons... wore number 11 in the McDonald's Basketball Open in Madrid, when his squad played against Boston... played 21 minutes against Boston on 10/21/88 in Madrid, and grabbed 4 rebounds with 4 points (2-3 field goals)... came to Boston to see the Celtics-Warriors game on 11/16/88... played for Aris of Thesalonika (Greece) in 1989-90; that team advanced to the European Final Four.

PERSONAL: Stojko Vrankovic and his wife Lola have two daughters, Matea (2/7/88) and Andrea (10/1/89)... his occupation in Yugoslavia was a technician... names Magic Johnson and Larry Bird as his favorite basketball players, and mentions Bird as the best he has ever seen... is a fan of boxer Mike Tyson... lists his choice recreational sports as soccer, team handball, and swimming... listens to disco music... has an incredible 37-inch vertical jump... shoe size is 16.

TOP REGULAR SEASON PERFORMANCES

Points
7 vs. New Jersey (4-4-91)
5 at Detroit (1-21-91)
5 vs. Dallas (1-6-91)

Rebounds
7 at Detroit (1-21-91)
4 vs. Orlando (1-30-91)
4 vs. Atlanta (4-21-91)

Assists
1 four times

REGULAR SEASON RECORD

Year	Team	G	Min	FGM	FGA	Pct.	FTM	FTA	Pct.	Off	Def	Tot	Ast	PF-Dq	St	Bl	Pts	Avg
90-91	Bos.	31	166	24	52	.462	10	18	.556	15	36	51	4	43-1	1	29	58	1.9

Three-Point Field Goals: None attempted.

PLAYOFF RECORD

Year	Team	G	Min	FGM	FGA	Pct.	FTM	FTA	Pct.	Off	Def	Tot	Ast	PF-Dq	St	Bl	Pts	Avg
90-91	Bos.	1	4	1	1	1.000	0	0	.000	0	2	2	0	2-0	0	0	2	2.0

Three-Point Field Goals: None attempted.

SEASON/CAREER HIGHS

	FGM	FGA	FTM	FTA	REB	AST	ST	BL	PTS
1990-91/Regular Season	3/3	5/5	2/2	4/4	7/7	1/1	1/1	4/4	7/7
1991/Playoffs	1/1	1/1	0/0	1/1	2/2	0/0	0/0	0/0	2/2

JOHN BAGLEY

Birthdate: April 23, 1960
Birthplace: Bridgeport, CT
High School: Warren Harding High (CT)
College: Boston College '83
Height: 6-0
Weight: 192
NBA Experience: 9 Years

HOW ACQUIRED: Traded by New Jersey to Boston for 1991 and 1993 second-round draft choices on October 5, 1989.

1990-91 SEASON: Underwent successful arthroscopic surgery on his right knee at the Cleveland Clinic in Cleveland on 3/14... the surgery was performed by Dr. John A. Bergfeld in consultation with Dr. Arnold Scheller... the surgery found a cartilage fracture of the bone in his right knee and the repair was performed successfully... spent the entire 1990-91 regular season on the injured list... began the season on the IL due to tendinitis of the right knee... did not make the playoff roster... **1991 Playoffs:** was not activated.

PROFESSIONAL CAREER: Drafted by Cleveland on the first-round of the 1982 draft as an undergraduate, the 12th pick overall... in his third NBA season, he accomplished a career best 35 points on February 4, 1985... finished fourth among assists leaders in 1985-86, averaging a team record 9.4 per game... traded by Cleveland (with Keith Lee) to New Jersey for Darryl Dawkins and James Bailey on October 8, 1987... in only five seasons with the Cavaliers, he became their all-time assists leader with 2,311... passed the 5,000 career scoring mark in 1988-89 and surpassed the 3,000 career assists total in the same season... in 1988-89, he started the first 20 games; later in the

season, he spent 13 games on the injured list with a sprained left ankle ... registered his lone double-double of his first Celtics' season on opening night... started 17 times in 1989-90; season was abbreviated due to a separated left shoulder in November, and a right hamstring strain in February.

COLLEGE CAREER: Passed up his final year of eligibility to enter the NBA draft... a three-year starter at Boston College, he led the team in scoring each season... finished fourth on the all-time BC scoring list... named Big East Player of the Year for the 1980-81 campaign... set Big East records for most points (30) and most free throws (16) in one game (January 16, 1981 vs. Villanova)... points per game increased in each season, career average was 17.9.

PERSONAL: John Edward Bagley is single... is one of eight children... founded the Bagley-Walden Foundation with the purpose of helping young people develop strategies for success through the utilization of athletic and academic programs... in the past, he has returned to Bridgeport during the summer to run a series of camps... at times, he's purchased a block of tickets for charitable use, known as the Bagley Bunch... names George Gervin as the greatest basketball player he has seen... most memorable Christmas: receiving his first pair of Pro Keds' sneakers at the age of ten... favorite pregame meal is pancakes... likes playing tennis... enjoys Bill Cosby... would like to get involved in coaching upon the conclusion of playing career... majored in Sociology... shoe size is 12.

CAREER HIGHS: 35 points at Washington (2-4-85)
11 rebounds at Boston (2-6-85)
19 assists at Dallas (3-16-85)

TOP REGULAR SEASON PERFORMANCES

Points	Rebounds	Assists
14 vs. Phila at Htfd (11-14-89)	6 at Houston (2-13-90)	16 vs. Milwaukee (11-3-89)
13 vs. Milwaukee (11-3-89)	5 at Miami (4-7-90)	14 at Chicago (4-17-90)
12 vs. Minnesota (11-17-89)	5 vs. Detroit (3-30-90)	13 vs. Atlanta (11-10-89)
11 two times	4 two times	1 vs. New Jersey (4-4-90)

NBA CAREER RECORD

Year	Team	G	Min	FGM	FGA	Pct.	FTM	FTA	Pct	Off	Def	Tot	Ast	PF-Dq	St	Bl	Pts	Avg
82-83	Clev	68	990	161	373	.432	64	84	.762	17	79	96	167	74-0	54	5	386	5.7
83-84	Clev	76	1712	257	607	.423	157	198	.793	49	107	156	333	113-1	78	4	673	8.9
84-85	Clev	81	2401	338	693	.488	125	167	.749	54	237	291	697	132-0	129	5	804	9.9
85-86	Clev	78	2472	366	865	.423	170	215	.791	76	199	275	735	165-1	122	10	911	11.7
86-87	Clev	72	2182	312	732	.426	113	136	.831	55	197	252	379	114-0	91	7	768	10.7
87-88	N.J.	82	2774	393	896	.439	148	180	.822	61	196	257	479	162-0	110	10	981	12.0
88-89	N.J.	68	1642	200	481	.416	89	123	.724	36	108	144	391	117-0	72	5	500	7.4
89-90	Bos	54	1095	100	218	.459	29	39	.744	26	63	89	296	77-0	40	4	230	4.3
90-91	Bos.			INJURED														
TOTALS:		579	15268	2127	4865	.437	895	1142	.784	374	1186	1560	3477	954-2	696	50	5253	9.1

Three-Point Field Goals: 1982-83, 0-for-14; 1983-84, 2-for-17 (.118); 1984-85, 3-for-26 (.115); 1985-86, 9-for-37 (.243); 1986-87, 31-for-103 (.301); 1987-88, 47-for-161 (.292); 1988-89, 11-for-54 (.204); 1989-90, 1-for-18 (.056).
Totals: 104-for-430 (.242).

PLAYOFF RECORD

Year	Team	G	Min	FGM	FGA	Pct.	FTM	FTA	Pct	Off	Def	Tot	Ast	PF-Dq	St	Bl	Pts	Avg
84-85	Clev	4	168	22	56	.393	7	10	.700	1	15	16	40	7-0	10	0	51	12.8
89-90	Bos	5	70	8	15	.533	3	4	.750	3	1	4	17	9-0	4	1	19	3.8
90-91	Bos.			INJURED														
TOTALS:		9	238	30	71	.423	10	14	.714	4	16	20	57	16-0	14	1	70	7.8

Three-Point Field Goals: 1984-85, 0-for-3; 1989-90, 0-for-1 (.000); 1990-91, 0-for-0 (.000).
Totals: 0-for-4 (.000).

SEASON/CAREER HIGHS

	FGM	FGA	FTM	FTA	REB	AST	ST	BL	PTS
1990-91/Regular Season	0/16	0/21	0/10	0/12	0/11	0/19	0/6	0/2	0/35
1991/Playoffs	0/11	0/19	0/4	0/6	0/7	0/15	0/5	0/1	0/22

DAVE POPSON

Birthdate: May 17, 1964
Birthplace: Kingston, PA
High School: Bishop O'Reilly (PA)
College: North Carolina '87
Height: 6-10
Weight: 230
NBA Experience: 2 Years

HOW ACQUIRED: Signed as a free agent on August 17, 1990.

1990-91 SEASON: Made the Celtics squad after failing to do so during the 1989 preseason... waived by Boston on 12/24, only to be re-signed on 12/27... placed on the injured list on 3/4 due to a degenerative bone spur in the mid-area of his left foot... played in 3 straight games from 2/3-2/7, a personal first... dressed, but did not play on 1/30 vs. Orlando due to a sore left foot... scored 6 points (3-3 fgs) in 9 minutes vs. New York on 1/2... best game is 11/30 vs. Washington, as he tallied 10 points (4-4, 2-2) in only 4 minutes... DNP-CD 38 times... **1991 Playoffs:** was not eligible to play.

PROFESSIONAL CAREER: Drafted by the Detroit Pistons on the fourth-round of the 1987 draft, the 88th choice overall... played with Monaco (French first division) in 1987 for former UCLA star Bill Sweek, where he shot 53% and led the team in rebounding waived by the Pistons on 11/1/88, claimed off waivers by the Clippers two days later, then waived by the LAC on 11/14/88... re-signed with the Clippers on 11/17/88 and appeared in 10 games; scored 23 points (11-25, 1-2), with 16 rebounds, 6 assists, and 2 blocks in 68 minutes... waived on 12/8/88 by the LAC, re-signed by the same club on 1/8/89 to a 10-day contract that expired 1/18/89... signed by the Albany Patroons of the CBA... for Albany, he played in 14 games, 300 minutes, scored 154 points (11.0 average), made 69 of 127 field goals (.543), made 16 of 28 free throws (.571), and totalled 85 rebounds (6.1)... appeared in two postseason contests with the Patroons... became a member of the Miami Heat, on 3/22/89, when Pat Cummings was placed on the injured list; signed consecutive 10-day contracts which expired on 4/12/89... signed a pact for the remainder of the season on 4/12/89... with the Heat, he played 7 games and scored 11 points (5-15, 1-2) with 11 rebounds in 38 minutes... signed as a free agent by the Celtics on September 6th, 1989... participated with the Celtics during the 1989 preseason before being waived on October 31, 1989 (the last cut with Scooter Barry)... played in nine games with Albany in 1989-90, before being placed on the injured list on December 8, 1989 when he decided to play in Europe.

COLLEGE CAREER: Played in 134 contests, and scored 760 points for a 5.7 ppg... grabbed 382 total rebounds for an average of 2.9 per game... made 52.1% of his field goals (329-632), and 102 of his 135 fts for a 75.6%.

PERSONAL: David Gerard Popson is married, wife's name is Carolyn... lists his father as his greatest influence on his athletic career... his dad was the head football coach at Bishop O'Reilly in Kingston, PA for 25 years... lists his favorite foods as anything his mom makes... James Worthy and Michael Jordan are the basketball players he admires the most, while Dick Butkus of football's Chicago Bears was his top athlete... chosen pregame meal is spaghetti... returns to Pennsylvania in the summer... shoe size is 15.

CAREER HIGHS: 4 rebounds three times
2 assists three times

TOP REGULAR SEASON PERFORMANCES

Points	Rebounds	Assists
10 vs. Washington (11-30-90)	2 five times	1 two times
6 vs. New York (1-2-91)		

NBA RECORD

Year	Team	G	Min	FGM	FGA	Pct.	FTM	FTA	Pct.	Off	Def	Tot	Ast	PF-Dq	St	Bl	Pts	Avg
88-89	LAC/Mi	17	106	16	40	.400	2	4	.500	12	15	27	8	17-0	1	3	34	2.0
90-91	Bos.	19	64	13	32	.406	9	10	.900	7	7	14	2	12-0	1	2	35	1.8
TOTALS:		36	170	29	72	.403	11	14	.786	19	22	41	10	29-0	2	5	69	1.9

Three-Point Field Goals: None attempted.

SEASON/CAREER HIGHS

	FGM	FGA	FTM	FTA	REB	AST	ST	BL	PTS
1990-91/Regular Season	4/4	5/13	3/3	4/4	2/4	1/2	1/1	1/1	10/10
1991/Playoffs	-/-	-/-	-/-	-/-	-/-	-/-	-/-	-/-	-/-

A.J. WYNDER

Birthdate: September 11, 1964
Birthplace: Bronx, NY
College: Fairfield '87
Height: 6-2
Weight: 180
Position: Guard
NBA Experience: 1 Year

HOW ACQUIRED: Signed as a free agent on April 12, 1991.

1990-91 SEASON: Placed on the injured list due to a right groin pull on 4/21... signed by Boston to a contract for the remainder of the season on 4/12... originally signed to a 10-day contract with Boston on 3/25, but that expired on 4/3; he was not offered a new contract due to Derek Smith's activation... 10+ mins once ... DNP-CD 3 times...
1991 Playoffs: was not activated... in the CBA, he played in 53 games for the Cedar Rapids Silver Bullets (15) and the Quad City Thunder (38) combined ... he led the league with 161 steals and was named to the All-Defensive First Team... was named CBA Player of the Week for the period ending March 9 after averaging 24.5 points, 16.0 assists and shooting .676 (23-34) from the field as his squad entered first place in their division... led the Thunder in assists (9.5) and steals (3.0) during the season and he rejoined the team in between his Celtics' stints... made 23 of 77 (.299) 3-pointers during the season, and tallied 1,997 minutes, 325-667 (.487) field goals, 178-215 (.828) free throws, 196 rebounds, 465 assists, 6 blocks, 161 steals, and 851 points... in the CBA playoffs, he participated in 6 contests, and registered 210 minutes, 36-75 (.480) field goals, 17-18 (.944) free throws, 17 rebounds, 40 assists, 1 block, 15 steals, and 91 points; he also made 2 of 7 3-pointers... activated by the Erie Wave of the World Basketball League on June 4th.

PROFESSIONAL CAREER: Undrafted by an NBA team, he played in 54 games for the Continental Basketball Association's Wyoming Wildcatters in his inaugural professional season, 1987-88... tallied 1,256 minutes, shot .449 (150-334) from the field, .813 (109-134) from the free throw line, 120 rebounds, and 172 assists in that rookie season... in 1988-89, he played in 52 games for the CBA's Cedar Rapids Silver Bullets, and averaged 12.6 points... in 1989-90, he split his playing time with St. Etienne of France, and the Erie Wave (7 games) of the WBL.

COLLEGE CAREER: Is the only Fairfield University product to advance to the NBA... also played basketball at the University of Massachusetts... saw 14 minutes in two early season games in 1982-83 before leaving UMass... transferred to Fairfield and started 113 of his final 118 games for the Stags... in 1987, he hit a buzzer-beating three-point field goal to send the MAAC championship game into overtime; the Stags won in overtime against Iona and advanced to the NCAA tourney... ranked ninth in Stags' history in points scored (1,313), third in assists (522) and first in games played (116).

PERSONAL: Arthur Wynder, Jr. is single... goes by the name of "A.J."... has residency in both Hampton, VA, and in Hempstead, NY... enjoyed the cuisine in France... his best friend is Troy Bradford, a member of the Harlem Globetrotters chief opponent the Washington Generals... has a marketing degree... shoe size is 10 and a half.

TOP REGULAR SEASON PERFORMANCES

Points	Rebounds	Assists
4 at New Jersey (4-2-91)	2 at Philadelphia (4-18-91)	3 at Philadelphia (4-18-91)
3 at Philadelphia (4-18-91)	1 vs. New York (4-14-91)	3 at Cleveland (4-19-91)
3 at Detroit (4-16-91)		2 at Detroit (4-16-91)

NBA RECORD

Year	Team	G	Min	FGM	FGA	Pct.	FTM	FTA	Pct.	Off	Def	Tot	Ast	PF-Dq	St	Bl	Pts	Avg
90-91	Bos.	6	39	3	12	.250	6	8	.750	1	2	3	8	1-0	1	0	12	2.0

Three-Point Field Goals: 1990-91, 0-for-1 (.000).

SEASON/CAREER HIGHS

	FGM	FGA	FTM	FTA	REB	AST	ST	BL	PTS
1990-91/Regular Season	6/6	13/14	2/3	2/3	4/5	8/8	3/3	1/1	13/13
1991/Playoffs	0/0	0/0	0/0	0/0	0/0	0/0	0/0	0/0	0/0

DEREK SMITH

Birthdate: November 1, 1961
Birthplace: Hogansville, GA
High School: Hogansville High (GA)
College: Louisville '82
Height: 6-6
Weight: 218
NBA Experience: 8 Years

HOW ACQUIRED: Signed as a free agent on December 22, 1990.

1990-91 SEASON: Activated from the injured list for a second time during the season on April 21 and appeared in the season finale vs. Atlanta... placed on the injured list on 4/12 after his initial activation on 4/3... DNP-CD twice; his first action was on 4/4 vs. New Jersey... signed by Boston as a free agent during a rehabilitation period and was placed on the suspended list on 12/22... shifted to the injured list on 12/27... **1991 Playoffs:** played in 10 games, including his best outing - Game Five vs. Indiana in which he tallied 12 points in 22 minutes, and played tenacious defense against Chuck Person.

PROFESSIONAL CAREER: Drafted by Golden State on the second-round of the 1982 draft, the 35th player taken overall... waived by the Warriors on September 8, 1983 after appearing in just 27 games as a rookie... signed by the San Diego Clippers as a free agent on September 13, 1983, and played better than two seasons with that organization... had his best professional season in 1984-85, when he ranked in the top five among starting guards in scoring, rebounding, field goal percentage, and blocks... had 5 blocks at Utah on April 9, 1985... contracted mononucleosis on Christmas Day, 1985, limiting his appearances to 11 games in his final season with the Los Angeles

Clippers... part of a major trade on August 19, 1986, as the Clippers traded Smith, Junior Bridgeman, and Franklin Edwards to the Sacramento Kings for Larry Drew, Mike Woodson, a 1988 1st round draft choice and a 1989 2nd round draft choice... recorded 7 steals vs. Denver on March 7, 1988... after two-plus seasons in Sacramento, the Kings waived him on February 7, 1989... signed by Philadelphia as a free agent six days later... missed the final four games of the 1989-90 regular season and nine playoff games due to tendonitis of his left knee... scored 10+ points 35 times in 1989-90... underwent left knee surgery in September, 1990.

COLLEGE CAREER: A standout player throughout his four years at Louisville... named to the Metro Conference Tournament Team in each of his last three seasons... was co-Metro Player of the Year in 1980-81... led the Cardinals in scoring as a senior, and in rebounding and scoring as a junior... member of the 1979-80 NCAA Champions... concluded his collegiate play as the school's second top scorer ever with 1,826 points in 131 games... made .577 (722-1,251) of his field goals.

PERSONAL: Derek Ervin Smith and his wife Monica have two children, a daughter Sydney (11/30/85) and a son Nolan (7/25/88)... favorite basketball player was Julius Erving... favorite athlete was Atlanta Braves' hurler Phil Niekro... favorite baseball team is the Cincinnati Reds... actively involved in a number of charities... enjoys listening to music and likes to fish... lists the 1965 Thunderbird as his favorite car... returns to Kentucky in the summer.

CAREER HIGHS: 41 points vs. Kansas City (4-3-85)
11 rebounds at Houston (3-13-84)
vs. Denver (11-5-84)
at Phoenix (1-11-85)
10 assists at LA Lakers (11-16-86)

TOP REGULAR SEASON PERFORMANCES

Points	Rebounds	Assists
4 vs. New Jersey (4-4-91)	0	4 vs. New Jersey (4-4-91)

NBA RECORD

Year	Team	G	Min	FGM	FGA	Pct.	FTM	FTA	Pct.	Off	Def	Tot	Ast	PF-Dq	St	Bl	Pts	Avg
82-83	G.S.	27	154	21	51	.412	17	25	.680	10	28	38	2	40-0	0	4	59	2.2
83-84	S.D.	61	1297	238	436	.546	123	163	.755	54	116	170	82	165-2	33	22	600	9.8
84-85	LAC	80	2762	682	1271	.537	400	504	.794	174	253	427	216	317-8	77	52	1767	22.1
85-86	LAC	11	339	100	181	.552	58	84	.690	20	21	41	31	35-2	9	13	259	23.5
86-87	Sac.	52	1658	338	757	.447	178	228	.781	60	122	182	204	184-3	46	23	863	16.6
87-88	Sac.	35	899	174	364	.478	87	113	.770	35	68	103	89	108-2	21	17	443	12.7
88-89	Sac/Ph	65	1295	216	496	.435	129	188	.686	61	106	167	128	164-4	43	23	568	8.7
89-90	Phil	75	1405	261	514	.508	130	186	.699	62	110	172	109	198-2	35	20	668	8.9
90-91	Bos.	2	16	1	4	.250	3	4	.750	0	0	0	5	3-0	1	1	5	2.5
TOTALS:		408	9825	2031	4074	.499	1125	1495	.753	476	824	1300	866	1214-23	265	175	5232	12.8

Three-Point Field Goals: 1982-83, 0-for-2 (.000); 1983-84, 1-for-6 (.167); 1984-85, 3-for-19 (.158); 1985-86, 1-for-2 (.500); 1986-87, 9-for-33 (.373); 1987-88, 8-for-23 (.348); 1988-89, 7-for-31 (.226); 1989-90, 16-for-36 (.444); 1990-91, 0-for-1 (.000).
Totals: 45-for-153 (.294).

PLAYOFF RECORD

Year	Team	G	Min	FGM	FGA	Pct.	FTM	FTA	Pct.	Off	Def	Tot	Ast	PF-Dq	St	Bl	Pts	Avg
88-89	Phil	3	48	9	14	.643	1	2	.500	2	5	7	3	9-0	1	0	19	6.3
89-90	Phil	1	15	5	8	.625	1	2	.500	0	0	0	1	3-0	1	0	11	11.0
90-91	Bos.	10	86	9	21	.429	11	14	.786	2	7	9	5	20-0	3	1	29	2.9
TOTALS:		14	149	23	43	.535	13	18	.722	4	12	16	9	32-0	5	1	59	4.2

Three-Point Field Goals: 1989-90, 0-for-1 (.000); 1990-91, 0-for-1 (.000).
Totals: 0-for-2 (.000).

SEASON/CAREER HIGHTS

	FGM	FGA	FTM	FTA	REB	AST	ST	BL	PTS
1990-91/Regular Season	1/14	3/26	2/13	2/17	0/11	4/10	1/7	1/5	4/41
1991/Playoffs	5/5	9/9	4/4	4/4	3/3	2/2	1/1	1/1	12/1

RICK FOX

Birthdate: July 24, 1969
Birthplace: Toronto, Ontario
High School: Warsaw High (Warsaw, IN)
College: North Carolina '91
Height: 6-7
Weight: 231
NBA Experience: Rookie

HOW ACQUIRED: Celtics first-round draft choice in 1991... 24th pick overall.

1990-91 SEASON: Including tournaments, he played in 35 games as a senior... registered double digits in points in every game but three... scored 20+ points 11 times, including a season high of 26 against Clemson in just 28 minutes... 10+ rebounds 6 times, including a career best 15 against Virginia in the ACC Tournament... in the NCAA Tournament, he scored 13 points with nine rebounds and nine assists in the Tar Heels loss to Kansas... ended a 19-game 10+ point scoring streak when he scored 6 points against Eastern Michigan in the tourney... scored 19 points with seven rebounds in North Carolina's final tourney win, vs. Temple... overall, the Tar Heels were 4-1 in the tourney, beating Northeastern, Villanova, Eastern Michigan, and Temple before succumbing to Kansas in the semifinals; his point output ranged from 6-19 in those games... chosen to the East Regional All-Tournament Team... in the ACC Tournament, became the 11th player in North Carolina history to win the Everett Case Award as the ACC Tournament's Most Valuable Player... joined Larry Miller (1967 and 1968), Charlie Scott (1969), Bob McAdoo (1972) and James Worthy (1982) as the only Tar Heel players to win the ACC Tournament MVP award the same year in which they earned All-ACC First-Team honors... scored a tourney high 25 points in the ACC championship game win over Duke... made the First-Team All-ACC... led UNC in scoring (16.9 ppg), and steals (70).

COLLEGE CAREER: Tied a school record by playing in 140 games during his career; never missed a contest in four seasons... 13th all-time scorer at UNC with 1,703 points... all-time leader in steals with 197...scored a career best 26 points twice, asa senior against Clemson and on 12/30/89 vs. Colorado... registered double-doubles seven times, including five as a senior... named the team's MVP in his junior season... made 70 three-point field goals as a junior, third best in club history... registered double digits in points 28 times in 34 contests as a junior, and produced 10+ points in 14 straight games as a sophomore... during his second season, he tallied 25 points on opening night against Tennessee-Chattanooga... won the Butch Bennett Award as the team's most inspirational freshman player in 1987-88... as a frosh, he won the Mary Frances Andrews Award as the club's best field goal shooter... became one of eight players under Dean Smith to start in his first game, as the undermanned Carolina squad faced off against #1 Syracuse.

PERSONAL: Ulrick Fox is single... majored in Radio, Television and Motion Pictures... lists his hobby as golfing... admires NBA star James Worthy... favorite book is "The World's Greatest Salesman"... enjoys his mom's cooking, and also Mrs. Lee's carrot cake... favorite television show is "In Living Color"... favorite movie is "Presumed Innocent"... dedicated to his religion... attended high school in Indiana; Rick moved from Nassau, Bahamas where he lived with his parents Dianne and Ulrich.

COLLEGE RECORD

Year	Team	G	Min	FGM	FGA	Pct.	FTM	FTA	Pct.	Off	Def	Tot	Ast	PF-Dq	St
87-88	UNC	34	59	94	.628	15	30	.500	63	32	68-1	26	5	136	4.0
88-89	UNC	37	165	283	.583	83	105	.790	142	76	122-8	47	16	426	11.5
89-90	UNC	34	203	389	.522	75	102	.735	157	84	112-6	54	6	551	16.2
90-91	UNC	35	206	455	.453	111	138	.804	232	131	103-3	70	17	590	16.9
TOTALS:		140	633	1221	.518	284	375	.757	594	323	405-18	197	44	1703	12.2

Three-Point Field Goals: 1987-88, 3-for-9 (.333); 1988-89, 13-for-29 (.448); 1989-90, 70-for-160 (.438); 1990-91, 67-for-196 (.342).
Totals: 153-for-394 (.388).

RED AUERBACH

PRESIDENT

For the first four years of its existence, the Boston Celtics were a struggling operation at best, losing six times in every ten outings. Team Owner Walter Brown decided it would take a unique person, one of ingenuity and determination to steer the fortunes of his team. The search concluded with Red Auerbach, previously the Head Coach of the Washington Capitols and Tri-Cities Hawks. Although the Celtics were competitive for the first six years of the Auerbach regime, the NBA championship still eluded the franchise.

On April 20, 1956 Auerbach engineered an historic transaction by trading Ed Macauley and Cliff Hagan to St. Louis for the Hawks first-round pick who would be Bill Russell. This blockbuster move would spur the Celtics into the most dominant franchise in pro basketball history. Auerbach, who is still the winningest coach in NBA annals, coached the Celtics to nine NBA championships, including eight in succession from 1959-1966. Upon retiring as the team's Head Coach, Auerbach concentrated singularly on his duties as General Manager.

With his guidance and knowledge, the Celtics would continue to win. In 1968 and 1969, the Celtics would add two more titles. But after a down period in the early 70's, Auerbach restructured the team adding key personnel through trades and the draft, and ultimately would raise banners in 1974 and 1976. It was after these years that Auerbach would have his toughest test, as the late 1970's were a dismal period for the Celtics. Yet, Auerbach once again saved the franchise with the shrewd selection of Larry Bird in the 1978 draft. Although he would have to wait a year before Bird could become a Celtic due to the latter's collegiate standing, Auerbach sensed that Bird was the man to rejuvenate the proud organization. Five other teams had a shot at Bird, but all passed.

In 1981, Boston would again be home to the NBA championship trophy but not before Auerbach orchestrated another blockbuster trade, as he dealt the first pick in the 1981 draft to Golden State for Robert Parish and the third overall pick who would be Kevin McHale. The master had struck yet again, as Boston added titles in 1984 and 1986 with the keen additions of Danny Ainge and Dennis Johnson.

Auerbach has been the recipient of numerous distinguished awards and honors throughout his career. In 1968, he was enshrined in the Basketball Hall of Fame in Springfield, Massachusetts for his coaching successes. When the NBA chose its Silver Anniversary Team honoring the best of the league's first 25 years, Red was chosen as coach of that distinguished team. In 1982, he was elected to the Washington Hall of Stars, a Hall of Fame which involve people from all sports. Red was also honored as NBA Coach of the Year in 1965 and NBA Executive of the Year in 1980. Also, in that year, he was selected to the NBA's 35th Anniversary Team as "Greatest Coach in the History of the

NBA," by the PBWAA.

In 1985, The Red Auerbach Fund, the establishment of a fund in the great coach's name, was created to promote athletic, recreational and other youth development activities in Boston and throughout the Commonwealth of Massachusetts. January 4, 1985 will always be a special day in Red's heart and in Boston sports history as the Celtics' family saluted its patriarch by having the number two retired in his honor (emblematic as the second most important person in the organization's annals, after founder Walter Brown). Nine months later, on September 20, 1985 (Red's 68th birthday), a life-size sculpture of Auerbach was unveiled and placed in Boston's notorious Faneuil Hall Marketplace so the public would have a lasting tribute to this basketball genius and legend.

He has received six honorary degrees from various institutions. Red values such honors so much that he kept a previous commitment to American International College by delivering their commencement speech although it required him to be a no-show in the Boston Garden for the deciding game in the Celtics-Hawks best-of-seven thriller on May 22, 1988. AIC presented Auerbach with a Doctor of Humanities Honorary Degree. A week earlier, on May 15, he received a Doctor of Arts Honorary Degree from Stonehill College. He has also received Honorary Doctorate Degrees in Humane Letters from Franklin Pierce College on May 24, 1981, the University of Massachusetts (Boston) in 1982, and from Boston University on May 13, 1984. In 1986, Central New England College honored him with an Honorary Doctorate Degree in Business Administration.

Red is the author of five books. His first, Basketball for the Player, the Fan and Coach, has been translated into seven languages and is the largest-selling basketball book in print. His second book, Winning the Hard Way, was co-authored with Paul Sann. Then came the first of two publications written in conjunction with Joe Fitzgerald. Red Auerbach: An Autobiography was the title of that book. The more recent publication is, Red Auerbach On and Off the Court. In October, 1991, Auerbach's latest book, M.B.A.: Management by Auerbach was co-authored with Ken Dooley. In 1987, an excellent instructional video entitled, Winning Basketball,

became available to the public featuring the insight, thoughts and philosophy of Red and three-time NBA Most Valuable Player and Celtics' captain Larry Bird.

Auerbach has frequently been recognized for his many accomplishments in the world of basketball. But just as deserved is his recognition as one of the great organizational leaders in corporate America.

Born in Brooklyn, New York, Red attended Eastern District High School in that city, and attended Seth Low Junior College in New York and George Washington University in the District of Columbia. He played three years of college basketball at GW, and was the team's leading scorer and defensive specialist.

Red (9/20/17) and his wife Dorothy, live in Washington, D.C. The couple, married since 1941, are the proud parents of two daughters, Nancy, who is the deputy postmaster in the House of Representatives and is married to CNN anchorman Reid Collins, and Randy, who is Vice-President of Creative Affairs for Mel Brooks' Films in Hollywood. Red and Dorothy have one granddaughter, Julie, who is a student at GW and was recently married to Eric Fleiger.

Dave and Red.

DAVE GAVITT

SENIOR EXECUTIVE VICE PRESIDENT

After one season as the individual controlling the Boston Celtics, it became distinctively evident that Dave Gavitt was the breath of fresh air needed to revitalize the team's program. Every aspect of the organizational chart was untouched by the aura of Gavitt's input, whether it was redesigning the practice facility for a more professional appeal, dealing with the front office personnel in a contemporary nature, or adding his amazing mastery of the sport in the operational end. That is precisely why the marriage of Gavitt to the Celtics family was a tremendously effective union.

"I feel more comfortable with a full season under my belt," said Gavitt after his rookie campaign on the professional level. "However, my goal is similar to the Celtics goal of the past, and that is to bring the championship trophy back where it belongs - in Boston. I won't feel fully satisfied until we are all in Government Center Plaza with our fans celebrating our 17th title," uttered Gavitt.

When the NBA's premier corporation sought a new man to regulate the organization after its sudden failure in the 1990 Playoffs, Gavitt was the solitary choice to be given the complete authority and responsibility to all phases of the Celtics basketball operation. "I believe that we have landed one of the best basketball minds in the business," remarked Arnold Auerbach on Gavitt's initial day as a Celtic. Comparable citations continued from every source. From players to front office types to the Commissioner of the National Basketball Association, David Stern, who elucidated: "I've worked a lot with Dave, and I think he's got terrific basketball expertise. He's also a terrific person. He really cares about the game. Dave's been great for the game. I couldn't be happier for the Celtics, Dave, or the NBA."

The definitive New Englander, Gavitt is a native of Westerly, Rhode Island. He was raised in Peterborough, New Hampshire, and graduated from Peterborough High School in 1955. Four years later, he graduated from Dartmouth College where he received a diploma in History, and three varsity basketball and baseball letters.

From there, Gavitt became the possessor of an impressive administrative resume. Commencing in 1960 at Worcester (Mass.) Academy as the Assistant Basketball Coach and Baseball Coach, Gavitt continued with stops at Providence College (1962-66) as Assistant Basketball Coach and Tennis Coach, and Dartmouth College as Assistant Basketball Coach (for half of 1966-67, Head Coach for the remainder of the same season through 1968-69, where he compiled an 18-33 record); then came the site where his prominence was strengthened, Providence College.

From 1969-79, as the Friar's sideline leader (he was also the school's Director of Athletics from 1971-82), his teams were a combined 227-117, including the 1972-73 squad which advanced Cinderella-like to the NCAA Final Four. He

Gavitt speaks with Alan Cohen.

was voted New England Coach of the Year in 1968, 1971, 1972, 1973, and 1977. A splendid opportunity was bestowed to Gavitt when he was duly chosen Head Coach of the 1980 US Olympic basketball team.

But the most pivotal moment of his amateur career came as the Big East Conference Commissioner. As its originator, the Big East Conference went from a fledgling league in 1979 to a superior group of athletic institutions. Eight times, Big East schools represented the NCAA final four in Gavitt's tenure; those squads advanced to the championship title game six times, including victories in 1984 by Georgetown and 1985 by Villanova. Gavitt was responsible for a conference that evolved into one of the most prosperous and puissant during his direction. He negotiated television contracts peerlessly, evidenced by the continuous upward gross income throughout the league's existence.

Not one to rest on his laurels, Gavitt is currently the President of USA Basketball (term ends in 1992, after the Olympics in Barcelona). He was a member of the NCAA Basketball Tournament Committee from 1978-84, a committee he chaired from 1981-84. Gavitt also chaired that committee during the period of growth to a 64-team field, while also introducing the usage of domed stadiums to the Final Four. He has been the recipient of honorary degrees from Franklin Pierce, Providence College, and St. John's University.

May 30, 1990 marked the dawning of a new era for the dynasty-laden Celtics, as Gavitt took the reins of the club's future. A man who exudes personna grata, Gavitt's marvelous reputation has no boundaries whether on the personal or professional level.

Dave (10/26/37), and his wife Julie, have two children, Dan (24, a 1988 Dartmouth graduate and member of the basketball staff at PC), and Corey (23, a 1989 graduate of the University of North Carolina and a member of the basketball staff at the University of Maryland). The couple resides in

JAN VOLK

GENERAL MANAGER

With the commencement of the 1990-91 season, Jan Volk entered his third decade and 20th season as a member of the Boston Celtics' managerial staff. In that time, he has progressed through a variety of behind-the-scenes activities to his current role of Executive Vice-President and General Manager. Since being appointed to this position in 1984, Volk has been an instrumental figure in molding teams which have compiled a 396-178 (.690) regular season record, five Atlantic Division titles, three Eastern Conference crowns, and one NBA Championship, in 1986, arguably the finest professional basketball team of this era. Without Volk's craftiness and commitment, that unit's final result might have been different.

He has made many transactions that have strengthened the Celtics, and in some cases those moves have led to confounding reactions from baffled rivals. Volk has been accountable for the acquisitions, contractual negotiations, renegotiations, and ultimate signings of all current Celtics' players while maintaining a well-deserved reputation as the foremost authority on the NBA salary cap, a unique system of checks and balances designed to manage the escalating costs of players salaries in an attempt to limit the expenditures of operating a league franchise.

A native of Davenport, Iowa, Volk grew up in Newton, Massachusetts and spent his summers as a youth working at his father's summer camp in Marshfield, where Red Auerbach held the Celtics' rookie camp for over twenty years. He attended Newton North High School, graduated from Colby College in 1968 and received his Law Degree from Columbia University in 1971. After passing the Massachusetts Bar Exam in June of 1971, he began his full-time employment with the Celtics.

Starting as Director of Ticket Sales, Volk gradually broadened his areas of responsibility and experience. He took over the team's equipment purchases and travel arrangements, before becoming Business Manager. Slowly, he began to convince Auerbach that his legal expertise could be utilized in the negotiating and drafting of player contracts. In 1974, Volk became the team's Legal Counsel and in 1976 he was named Vice-President of the club. In 1981, he assumed the additional responsibilities of Assistant General Manager, before the promotion to his existing post on July 11, 1984.

Jan, his wife Lissa, and their two children, Shari (15) and Matthew (10), live in Wayland, Massachusetts. He approaches his various hobbies, furniture-building, photography, and US and European history with the same intensity as his management of the Celtics.

Gavitt and Volk confer.

CHRIS FORD

HEAD COACH

Although the Boston Celtics did not fulfill their annual goal of winning the NBA championship, Chris Ford's first season at the helm of the Green was punctuated by success. He molded an aging team that was on a downward spiral into an incredibly prosperous unit. Leading the Celtics to the Atlantic Division championship, their best record in three years and the fourth best record in the league, Ford was honored with a third-place finish in voting for the NBA's top coach. During his marvelous performance, he joined Ed Macauley, Billy Cunningham, and Pat Riley as the fourth rookie head coach in the All-Star Game. His Eastern Conference squad edged the West's best, 116-114.

Chris has been a member of the Celtics' family since 1978 as a player and then assistant coach, and has developed a reputation of intelligence, leadership, and spirited involvement in each game. These characteristics led to the June 12, 1990 announcement of his first head coaching assignment, as he became the eleventh Head Coach and the sixth former Celtics' player to lead the team.

Drafted in the second-round (the 17th pick overall by Detroit in 1972), after a distinguished collegiate career at Villanova (he was elected to the Wildcats' Hall of Fame in 1988), Chris spent his first six years in the NBA with the Detroit Pistons. A valuable contributor for the Motor City squad, he will forever be noted in Pistons' history because of his steal of an inbounds pass and eventual game-winning basket in Game Three of the Pistons-Bucks mini-series on April 17, 1976 once considered the top play in the club's history.

In the early stages of his seventh season in Motown, Ford was dealt to Boston with a second-round draft pick (Tracy Jackson) for Earl Tatum on October 18, 1978. He was voted the Most Valuable Player on the 1978-79 team. Then, in 1979, in what was the most impressive one-season turnaround recorded by any NBA team, Ford's value to the Celtics became more evident. On October 12, 1979, as the Green Machine hosted the Houston Rockets in what is best known as Larry Bird's first regular season game, Ford converted the NBA's initial three-point goal in the first year of the trifecta. He developed a reputation as one of the league's best three-point bombers, finishing second that season to Seattle's Fred Brown. Ford also became the fifth player to connect on a four-point play when he completed the feat on November 22, 1980 vs. Cleveland. He became Nate Archibald's backcourt partner throughout the Celtics' successful 1981 championship drive, then called it a career after the 1981-82 season.

Christopher Joseph Ford played ten years in the NBA, appeared in 794 regular season games, and averaged 9.2 points. Number 42 was an excellent three-point shooter, as he made 37.5% (126-for-336) of his shots, saw action in 58 playoff encounters and averaged 7.5 points.

When veteran broadcaster Johnny Most was sidelined with an illness during the 1982-83 season, Ford joined the announcing crew, adding his adroit commentary. He also did some volunteer coaching with the flourishing Boston College basketball program. Upon the completion of the BC season, Chris was offered a job at that school as an Assistant Coach to Gary Williams. However, Ford rejoined the Celtics on June 9, 1983 when K.C. Jones and Red Auerbach offered him a similar position on the professional level.

Ford ultimately engaged in two world championships within his first three years on the bench. He entered an elite group of Celtics' personnel (Bill Russell, Tom Heinsohn, and Jones) who have earned championship rings as both a player and coach with the 16-time World Champions.

Chris (1/11/49), his wife Kathy, and their four children, Chris (6/25/75), Katie (4/12/78), Anthony (5/13/82), and Michael (12/6/84) live in Lynnfield, Massachusetts during the season. The family makes Margate, New Jersey, their home during the summer months.

DON CASEY

ASSISTANT COACH

Don Casey joined the Boston Celtics' coaching staff on July 23, 1990 and the experience led to his most productive professional move ever.

Casey was the Head Coach at Temple University from 1973-74 through 1981-82, where he compiled an impressive record of 151-94 (.616). The Owls finished first or second in the East Coast Conference in his last seven years, and he posted 20 or more wins three times. He was twice voted East Coast Conference Coach of the Year and he led Temple to one NCAA postseason tournament and three NIT berths.

In 1982-83, Casey joined the NBA ranks as an Assistant Coach to Paul Westhead (Chicago Bulls), then became an assistant to Jim Lynam (Los Angeles Clippers) the following campaign. In 1984-85, Casey was a Head Coach in the Italian Professional League, then returned to the NBA's Clippers as an assistant under Don Chaney and Gene Shue for the next three-plus seasons.

On January 19, 1989, Casey became the Clippers' Head Coach, replacing Shue for the remainder of the 1988-89 season. Casey was subsequently signed for the 1989-90 season as the Clippers' top man on July 13, 1989, and continued in that capacity throughout the season. Casey's Clippers finished at 30-52, sixth place in the Pacific Division. The Clippers announced after the conclusion of the regular season that Casey's contract would not be renewed. He concluded his tenure as Clippers' Head Coach at 41-85.

Casey has developed a reputation in coaching against zone defenses, and has authored a book on the subject entitled, "Temple of Zones."

Casey was born in Collingwood, New Jersey, and attended high school at Catholic High in Camden, New Jersey. He graduated from Temple University in 1960 (did not

play collegiate basketball).

Don (6/17/37), and his wife Dwynne, have three children, Lee Ann (22), Michael (20), and Sean (19). During the off-season, the couple maintains a home in California, while living in Boston during the season.

JON JENNINGS

ASSISTANT COACH

When Chris Ford was appointed Head Coach of the Boston Celtics, one of his first tasks was the completion of his coaching staff. Ford proudly chose Jon Jennings, formerly the team's Video Coordinator/Scout to one position. That revelation was officially declared on July 17, 1990.

Jennings, a native of Richmond, Indiana, has an impressive resume of basketball experience. While attending Indiana University from 1981-85, Jennings served Head Coach Bob Knight in various roles during his sophomore and junior years.

In 1983, Jennings served as a summer intern with the Indiana Pacers. His duties included ticket sales, public relations, and assisting George Irvine, the club's Vice-President of Basketball Operations. Jennings acquired valuable knowledge in that last capacity coordinating all college, CBA, and NBA scouting. At the age of 20, Jennings was hired by Irvine, who brought him to Los Angeles to assist in coaching duties with the Pacers' summer league squad.

Upon Irvine's appointment to Indiana's head coaching position, Jennings began to scout and coordinate videos fulltime. Jennings had a bird's-eye view of Pacers' home games, and upon the completion of first-half action, would edit a two-minute tape used in the halftime discussion between players and coaches.

Jennings joined the NBA Champion Boston Celtics in the summer of 1986, working as the club's initial Video Coordinator. When Jim Rodgers was chosen the leader of the Green, Jennings' responsibilities increased as he scouted Boston's future opponents as well as college players. Jon also assumed the duties of keeping statistical charts, breaking down the opponents offensive and defensive patterns, and formulating this information into game plans.

Jennings is an active participant in the Genesis Fund, a provider for the specialized care and treatment of children born with genetic diseases,

birth defects, and mental retardation at the National Birth Defects Center.

Jon (10/2/62) is single and lives in West Peabody, MA. A devotee of Winston Churchill, Jennings lists his interests as history, politics, reading and painting.

RECORDS

CELTICS IN NAISMITH MEMORIAL BASKETBALL HALL OF FAME
at Springfield, Massachusetts

IN ORDER OF ELECTION:

Ed Macauley (1960)
Andy Phillip (1961)
John (Honey) Russell (1964)
Walter Brown (1965)
Bill Mokray (1965)
Alvin (Doggie) Julian (1967)
Arnold (Red) Auerbach (1968)
Bob Cousy (1970)
Bill Russell (1974)
Bill Sharman (1975)
Frank Ramsey (1981)
John Havlicek (1983)
Sam Jones (1983)
Tom Heinsohn (1985)
Bob Houbregs (1986)
Pete Maravich (1986)
Clyde Lovellette (1987)
K.C. Jones (1988)
Dave Bing (1989)
Pete Maravich (1989)
Dave Cowens (1991)
Nate (Tiny) Archibald (1991)

RETIRED CELTICS NUMBERS

1 — Walter Brown
2 — Arnold (Red) Auerbach
6 — Bill Russell
10 — Jo Jo White
14 — Bob Cousy
15 — Tom Heinsohn
16 — Tom (Satch) Sanders
17 — John Havlicek
18 — Dave Cowens
    Jim Loscutoff*
19 — Don Nelson
21 — Bill Sharman
22 — Ed Macauley
23 — Frank Ramsey
24 — Sam Jones
25 — K.C. Jones

* Loscutoff's jersey was retired, but number 18 was kept active for Dave Cowens.

CELTICS ON ALL-NBA TEAM
(Selected by the media)

Player	1st Team	2nd Team	3rd Team	Total
Bob Cousy	10	2	0	12
John Havlicek	4	7	0	11
Bill Russell	3	8	0	11
Larry Bird	9	1	0	10
Bill Sharman	4	3	0	7
Ed Macauley	3	1	0	4
Tom Heinsohn	0	4	0	4
Dave Cowens	0	3	0	3
Sam Jones	0	3	0	3
Jo Jo White	0	2	0	2
Kevin McHale	1	0	0	1
Ed Sadowski	1	0	0	1
Nate Archibald	0	1	0	1
Robert Parish	0	1	2	3

INDIVIDUAL AWARDS

NBA EXECUTIVE OF THE YEAR
(Originated in 1972-73; selected by The Sporting News)
1979-80 Red Auerbach

NBA COACH OF THE YEAR
(Originated in 1962-63; selected by the media)
1964-65 Red Auerbach
1972-73 Tom Heinsohn
1979-80 Bill Fitch

NBA MOST VALUABLE PLAYER
(Originated in 1955-56; selected by NBA players)

1956-57	Bob Cousy
1957-58	Bill Russell
1960-61	Bill Russell
1961-62	Bill Russell
1962-63	Bill Russell
1964-65	Bill Russell
1972-73	Dave Cowens
1983-84	Larry Bird
1984-85	Larry Bird
1985-86	Larry Bird

PLAYOFFS' MOST VALUABLE PLAYER
(Originated in 1969; selected by Sport magazine)

1974	John Havlicek
1976	Jo Jo White
1981	Cedric Maxwell
1984	Larry Bird
1986	Larry Bird

CELTICS ON NBA'S 35TH ANNIVERSARY TEAM

(Chosen in 1980 to honor the top performers in the league's first 35 seasons.)

Coach: Arnold (Red) Auerbach

Players: Bob Cousy
John Havlicek
Bill Russell*

* Russell voted the league's greatest all-time player. (In all 11 players were chosen. The other eight: Kareem Abdul-Jabbar, Elgin Baylor, Wilt Chamberlain, Julius Erving, George Mikan, Bob Pettit, Oscar Robertson and Jerry West.)

CELTICS ON NBA'S SILVER ANNIVERSARY TEAM

(Chosen in 1971 to honor the top performers in the league's first 25 seasons.)

Coach: Arnold (Red) Auerbach

Players: Bob Cousy
Bill Russell
Bill Sharman
Sam Jones

(In all 10 players were chosen. The other six: George Mikan, Bob Pettit, Dolph Schayes, Paul Arizin, Bob Davies and Joe Fulks.)

NBA ROOKIE OF THE YEAR

(Originated in 1952-53; selected by the media)

1956-57 Tom Heinsohn
1970-71 Dave Cowens
(shared with Portland's Geoff Petrie)
1979-80 Larry Bird

NBA ALL-DEFENSIVE TEAM

(Originated in 1968-69; selected by the coaches)

1968-69	Bill Russell (1st team)
	John Havlicek (2nd team)
	Tom Sanders (2nd team)
1969-70	John Havlicek (2nd team)
1970-71	John Havlicek (2nd team)
1971-72	John Havlicek (1st team)
	Don Chaney (2nd team)
1972-73	John Havlicek (1st team)
	Don Chaney (2nd team)
	Paul Silas (2nd team)
1973-74	John Havlicek (1st team)
	Don Chaney (2nd team)
1974-75	John Havlicek (1st team)
	Paul Silas (1st team)
	Don Chaney (2nd team)
	Dave Cowens (2nd team)
1975-76	Dave Cowens (1st team)
	John Havlicek (1st team)
	Paul Silas (1st team)
1979-80	Dave Cowens (2nd team)
1981-82	Larry Bird (2nd team)
1982-83	Larry Bird (2nd team)
	Kevin McHale (2nd team)
1983-84	Larry Bird (2nd team)
	Dennis Johnson (2nd team)
1984-85	Dennis Johnson (2nd team)
1985-86	Kevin McHale (1st team)
	Dennis Johnson (2nd team)
1986-87	Kevin McHale (1st team)
	Dennis Johnson (1st team)
1987-88	Kevin McHale (1st team)
1988-89	Kevin McHale (2nd team)
1989-90	Kevin McHale (2nd team)

NBA SIXTH MAN

(Originated in 1982-83; selected by the media)

1983-84 Kevin McHale
1984-85 Kevin McHale
1985-86 Bill Walton

NBA ALL-ROOKIE TEAM

(Originated in 1962-63; selected by the coaches)

1962-63 John Havlicek
1969-70 Jo Jo White
1970-71 Dave Cowens
1979-80 Larry Bird
1980-81 Kevin McHale
1988-89 Brian Shaw (2nd team)
1990-91 Dee Brown

McHale won the Sixth Man Award for two seasons.

BOSTON CELTICS' COACHES

Year	Coach	Regular Season		Playoffs	
		Won	Lost	Won	Lost
1946-47	John (Honey) Russell	22	38	—	—
1947-48	John (Honey) Russell	20	28	1	2
1948-49	Alvin (Doggy) Julian	25	35	—	—
1949-50	Alvin (Doggy) Julian	22	46	—	—
1950-51	Arnold (Red) Auerbach	39	30	0	2
1951-52	Arnold (Red) Auerbach	39	27	1	2
1952-53	Arnold (Red) Auerbach	46	25	3	3
1953-54	Arnold (Red) Auerbach	42	30	2	4
1954-55	Arnold (Red) Auerbach	36	36	3	4
1955-56	Arnold (Red) Auerbach	39	33	1	2
*1956-57	Arnold (Red) Auerbach	44	28	7	3
1957-58	Arnold (Red) Auerbach	49	23	6	5
*1958-59	Arnold (Red) Auerbach	52	20	8	3
*1959-60	Arnold (Red) Auerbach	59	16	5	
*1960-61	Arnold (Red) Auerbach	57	22	8	2
*1961-62	Arnold (Red) Auerbach	60	20	8	6
*1962-63	Arnold (Red) Auerbach	58	22	8	5
*1963-64	Arnold (Red) Auerbach	59	21	8	2
*1964-65	Arnold (Red) Auerbach	62	18	8	4
*1965-66	Arnold (Red) Auerbach	54	26	11	6
1966-67	Bill Russell	60	21	4	5
*1967-68	Bill Russell	54	28	12	7
*1968-69	Bill Russell	48	34	12	6
1969-70	Tom Heinsohn	34	48	—	—
1970-71	Tom Heinsohn	44	38	—	—
1971-72	Tom Heinsohn	56	26	5	6
1972-73	Tom Heinsohn	68	14	7	6
*1973-74	Tom Heinsohn	56	26	12	6
1974-75	Tom Heinsohn	60	22	6	5
*1975-76	Tom Heinsohn	54	28	12	6
1976-77	Tom Heinsohn	44	38	5	4
1977-78	Tom Heinsohn	11	23		
	Thomas (Satch) Sanders	21	27	—	—
1978-79	Thomas (Satch) Sanders	2	12		
	Dave Cowens	27	41	—	—
1979-80	Bill Fitch	61	21	5	4
*1980-81	Bill Fitch	62	20	12	5
1981-82	Bill Fitch	63	19	7	5
1982-83	Bill Fitch	56	26	2	5
*1983-84	K.C. Jones	62	20	15	8
1984-85	K.C. Jones	63	19	13	8
*1985-86	K.C. Jones	67	15	15	3
1986-87	K.C. Jones	59	23	13	10
1987-88	K.C. Jones	57	25	9	—
1988-89	Jimmy Rodgers	42	40	0	3
1989-90	Jimmy Rodgers	52	30	2	3
1990-91	Chris Ford	56	26	5	7
TOTALS	Eleven Coaches	2223	1254	264	180

*NBA Championships

COACHING RECORDS

(Boston only)

Coach	Regular Season Record	Playoff Record
John Russell	42-66 (.389)	1-2 (.333)
Alvin Julian	47-81 (.367)	0-0 (.000)
Red Auerbach	795-397 (.667)	90-58 (.608)
Bill Russell	162-83 (.661)	28-18 (.609)
Tom Heinsohn	427-263 (.619)	47-33 (.588)
Tom Sanders	23-39 (.371)	0-0 (.000)
Dave Cowens	27-41 (.397)	0-0 (.000)
Bill Fitch	242-86 (.738)	26-19 (.578)
K.C. Jones	308-102 (.751)	65-37 (.637)
Jim Rodgers	94-70 (.573)	2-6 (.250)
Chris Ford	56-26 (.683)	5-7 (.417)
TOTALS	2223-1254 (.639)	264-180 (.595)

CELTICS' OWNERSHIP

1946-1948:	Walter Brown/Boston Garden-Arena Corporation
1948-1950:	Walter Brown
1950-1964:	Walter Brown/Lou Pieri
1964-1965:	Lou Pieri/Marjorie Brown
1965-1968:	Marvin Kratter/National Equities
1968-1969:	Ballantine Brewery
1969-1971:	E. E. (Woody) Erdman/Trans-National Comm.
1971-1972:	Investors' Funding Corporation
1972-1974:	Bob Schmertz/Leisure Technology
1974-1975:	Bob Schmertz/Irv Levin
1975-1978:	Irv Levin
1978-1979:	John Y. Brown/Harry Mangurian Jr.
1979-1983:	Harry Mangurian Jr.
1983-present:	Don Gaston, Paul Dupee, Jr., Alan Cohen

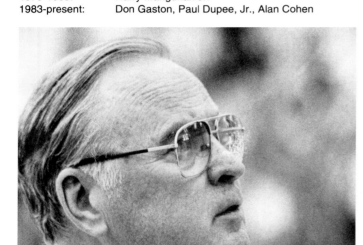

Scout Forddy Anderson.

Alan Cohen.

CELTICS' ASSISTANT COACHES

1946-47-1947-48:	Danny Silva
1948-49-1949-50:	Henry McCarthy
1949-50:	Art Spector
1972-73-1976-77:	John Killilea
1977-78:	Tom (Satch) Sanders
1978-79:	Bob MacKinnon
1977-78-1982-83:	K.C. Jones
1980-81-1987-88:	Jimmy Rodgers
1983-84-1989-90:	Chris Ford
1984-85-1987-88:	Ed Badger
1988-89-1989-90:	Lanny Van Eman
1990-91-present	Don Casey
1990-91-present	Jon P. Jennings

CELTICS' TRAINERS

1946-47-1957-58:	Harvey Cohn
1958-59-1966-67:	Edward (Buddy) LeRoux
1967-68-1970-71:	Joe DeLauri
1971-72-1978-79:	Frank Challant
1979-80-1986-87:	Ray Melchiorre
1987-88-present:	Ed Lacerte

Parish heads into his 16th NBA season.

CELTICS' CAREER LEADERS - REGULAR SEASON

GAMES

1. John Havlicek — 1,270
2. Bill Russell — 963
3. Bob Cousy — 917
4. Tom Sanders — 916
5. Robert Parish — 874
6. Don Nelson — 872
7. Sam Jones — 871
8. Larry Bird — 852
9. Kevin McHale — 844
10. Dave Cowens — 726

MINUTES

1. John Havlicek — 46,471
2. Bill Russell — 40,726
3. Larry Bird — 32,781
4. Bob Cousy — 30,131
5. Robert Parish — 28,560
6. Dave Cowens — 28,551
7. Kevin Mchale — 27,046
8. Jo Jo White — 26,770
9. Tom Sanders — 22,164
10. Bill Sharman — 21,793

POINTS

1. John Havlicek — 26,395
2. Larry Bird — 20,883
3. Bob Cousy — 16,955
4. Kevin McHale — 15,793
5. Sam Jones — 15,411
6. Bill Russell — 14,522
7. Dave Cowens — 13,192
8. Jo Jo White — 13,188
9. Robert Parish — 12,870
10. Bill Sharman — 12,287

AVERAGE POINTS (3 Yrs. Min.)

1. Larry Bird — 24.5
2. John Havlicek — 20.8
3. Ed Macauley — 18.9
4. Kevin McHale — 18.7
5. Tom Heinsohn — 18.6
6. Bob Cousy — 18.5
7. Jo Jo White — 18.3
8. Dave Cowens — 18.2
9. Bill Sharman — 18.1
10. Bailey Howell — 18.0

FIELD GOALS ATTEMPTED

1. John Havlicek — 23,930
2. Larry Bird — 16,576
3. Bob Cousy — 16,465
4. Sam Jones — 13,745
5. Bill Russell — 12,930
6. Jo Jo White — 12,782
7. Dave Cowens — 12,193
8. Tom Heinsohn — 11,787
9. Robert Parish — 11,182
10. Kevin McHale — 11,051

FREE THROWS ATTEMPTED

1. John Havlicek — 6,589
2. Bob Cousy — 5,753
3. Bill Russell — 5,614
4. Larry Bird — 4,389
5. Kevin McHale — 4,196
6. Robert Parish — 3,816
7. Sam Jones — 3,572
8. Ed Macauley — 3,518
9. Cedric Maxwell — 3,496
10. Bill Sharman — 3,451

FREE THROWS MADE

1. John Havlicek — 5,369
2. Bob Cousy — 4,621
3. Larry Bird — 3,810
4. Kevin McHale — 3,336
5. Bill Russell — 3,148
6. Bill Sharman — 3,047
7. Sam Jones — 2,869
8. Robert Parish — 2,784
9. Cedric Maxwell — 2,738
10. Ed Macauley — 2,724

FREE THROW PERCENTAGE (1,500 Att.)

1. Larry Bird — .883 (3810-4309)
2. Bill Sharman — .883 (3,047-3,451)
3. Larry Siegfried — .855 (1,500-1,755)
4. Jo Jo White — .833 (1,892-2,270)
5. John Havlicek — .815 (5,369-6,589)
6. Frank Ramsey — .804 (2,480-3,083)
7. Bob Cousy — .803 (4,621-5,753)
8. Sam Jones — .803 (2,869-3,572)
9. Kevin McHale — .795 (3386-4196)
10. Nate Archibald — .790 (1,401-1,773)

ASSISTS

1. Bob Cousy — 6,945
2. John Havlicek — 6,114
3. Larry Bird — 5,389
4. Bill Russell — 4,100
5. Jo Jo White — 3,686
6. Dennis Johnson — 3,001
7. K.C. Jones — 2,904
8. Dave Cowens — 2,828
9. Nate Archibald — 2,563
10. Sam Jones — 2,209

REBOUNDS

1. Bill Russell — 21,620
2. Dave Cowens — 10,170
3. Robert Parish — 9,064
4. Larry Bird — 8,540
5. John Havlicek — 8,007
6. Kevin McHale — 6,434
7. Tom Sanders — 5,798
8. Tom Heinsohn — 5,749
9. Bob Cousy — 4,781
10. Don Nelson — 4,517

FIELD GOALS MADE

1. John Havlicek — 10,513
2. Larry Bird — 8,238
3. Sam Jones — 6,271
4. Robert Parish — 6,243
5. Kevin McHale — 6,209
6. Bob Cousy — 6,167
7. Bill Russell — 5,687
8. Jo Jo White — 5,648
9. Dave Cowens — 5,608
10. Tom Heinsohn — 4,773

FIELD GOAL PERCENTAGE (2,000 ATT.)

1. Kevin McHale — .562 (6209-11,051)
2. Cedric Maxwell — .559 (2,786-4,984)
3. Robert Parish — .551 (4,657-8,455)
4. Rick Robey — .510 (1,144-2,241)
5. Larry Bird — .497 (8,238-16,576)
6. Danny Ainge — .490 (2,266-4,621)
7. Gerald Henderson — .489 (1,467-3,002)
8. Don Nelson — .484 (3,717-7,672)
9. Bailey Howell — .480 (2,290-4,766)
10. Nate Archibald — .469 (1,567-3,338)

PERSONAL FOULS

1. John Havlicek — 3,281
2. Tom Sanders — 3,044
3. Dave Cowens — 2,783
4. Bill Russell — 2,592
5. Robert Parish — 2,562
6. Kevin McHale — 2,252
7. Tom Heisnohn — 2,454
8. Bob Cousy — 2,231
9. Larry Bird — 2,197
10. Frank Ramsey — 2,158

DISQUALIFICATIONS

1. Tom Sanders — 94
2. Frank Ramsey — 87
3. Dave Cowens — 86
4. Tom Heisnohn — 58
5. Robert Parish — 45
6. Bob Brannum — 42
7. Don Chaney — 40
8. Jim Loscutoff — 40
9. Cedric Maxwell — 32

CELTICS' INDIVIDUAL REGULAR-SEASON RECORDS

SCORING

60	Larry Bird vs Atlanta (at New Orleans)	March 12, 1985
56	Kevin McHale vs Detroit	March 3, 1985
53	Larry Bird vs Indiana	March 30, 1983
51	Sam Jones at Detroit	October 29, 1965
50	Larry Bird at Dallas	March 10, 1986
50	Larry Bird vs Atlanta	November 10, 1989
49	Larry Bird vs Washington	January 27, 1988
49	Larry Bird at Phoenix	February 15, 1988
48	Larry Bird vs Houston	March 17, 1985
48	Larry Bird vs Portland	January 27, 1985
48	Larry Bird vs Atlanta	December 9, 1984
47	Larry Bird vs New York	April 12, 1987
47	Larry Bird at Portland	February 14, 1986
47	Larry Bird vs Detroit	November 27, 1985
47	Larry Bird vs Milwaukee	April 12, 1985

FIELD GOALS MADE

22	Larry Bird vs New York	April 12, 1987
22	Larry Bird vs Atlanta (at New Orleans)	March 12, 1985
22	Kevin McHale vs Detroit	March 3, 1985
21	Larry Bird at Portland	February 14, 1986
21	Larry Bird vs Indiana	March 30, 1983
21	Sam Jones at Detroit	October 29, 1965
20	Larry Bird vs Atlanta	December 9, 1984
20	Larry Bird vs Washington	January 27, 1988
20	Danny Ainge vs Phoenix	December 9, 1988

FREE THROWS MADE

20	Nate Archibald vs Chicago	January 16, 1980
19	Cedric Maxwell vs New Jersey	January 14, 1979
19	John Havlicek vs Seattle	February 6, 1970
19	Frank Ramsey at Detroit	December 3, 1957
19	Bill Sharman at Philadelphia	March 8, 1956

ASSISTS

28	Bob Cousy vs Minneapolis	February 27, 1959
23	Nate Archibald vs Denver	February 5, 1982
21	Bob Cousy vs St Louis	December 21, 1960
19	Nate Archibald at San Antonio	October 23, 1979
19	Bob Cousy vs Cincinnati	February 19, 1963
19	Bob Cousy vs Syracuse	November 24, 1956
18	Nate Archibald at Seattle	December 16, 1982
18	Bob Cousy at New York	November 21, 1959
18	Bob Cousy vs New York	January 18, 1953

REBOUNDS

51	Bill Russell vs Syracuse	February 5, 1960
49	Bill Russell vs Philadelphia	November 16, 1957
49	Bill Russell vs Detroit	March 11, 1965
43	Bill Russell vs Los Angeles	January 20, 1963
41	Bill Russell vs Syracuse	February 12, 1958
41	Bill Russell vs San Francisco	March 14, 1965
40	Bill Russell vs Cincinnati	December 12, 1958
40	Bill Russell vs Philadelphia	February 12, 1961

OPPONENTS' INDIVIDUAL REGULAR SEASON RECORDS

SCORING

64	Elgin Baylor, at Minneapolis	November 8, 1959
62	Wilt Chamberlain, Philadelphia at Boston	January 14, 1962
55	Kareem Abdul-Jabbar, at Milwaukee	December 10, 1971
54	Dominique Wilkins, at Atlanta	February 3, 1987

FIELD GOALS MADE

27	Wilt Chamberlain, Philadelphia at Boston	January 14, 1962
25	Elgin Baylor, at Minneapolis	November 8, 1959
25	Wilt Chamberlain, Phil vs Boston at NY	February 23, 1960

FREE THROWS MADE

22	Richie Guerin, New York at Boston	February 11, 1961
20	Kareem Abdul-Jabbar, Milwaukee at Boston	March 8, 1970

ASSISTS

25	Kevin Porter, at Detroit	March 9, 1979
21	Clem Haskins, Chicago at Boston (OT)	December 6, 1969
21	Earvin Johnson, Laker at Boston	December 15, 1989

REBOUNDS

55	Wilt Chamberlain, at Philadelphia	November 24, 1960
43	Wilt Chamberlain, at Philadelphia	March 6, 1965
42	Wilt Chamberlain, at Philadelphia	January 15, 1960
42	Wilt Chamberlain, at Philadelphia	January 14, 1966
42	Wilt Chamberlain, at Los Angeles	March 7, 1969

Cousy on the move.

Bob Harris (13), Chuck Cooper (11) and Bill Sharman (21) reach for a rebound in a 1954 playoff game against Syracuse.

INDIVIDUAL PLAYOFF RECORDS

MOST POINTS
—Game	54	John Havlicek vs. Atlanta	April 1, 1973
—Half	30	Larry Bird vs. Detroit	April 30, 1985
		John Havlicek vs. Atlanta	April 1, 1973
—Quarter	24	Larry Bird vs. Atlanta	May 11, 1988
—Overtime	12	Bob Cousy at Syracuse	March 17, 1954

MOST FIELD GOALS MADE
—Game	24	John Havlicek vs. Atlanta	April 1, 1973
—Half	14	John Havlicek vs. Atlanta	April 1, 1973
—Quarter	10	Larry Bird vs. Atlanta	May 11, 1988

MOST FIELD GOALS ATTEMPTED
—Game	36	John Havlicek vs. Atlanta	April 1, 1973
—Half	21	Larry Bird vs. Detroit	May 8, 1985
—Quarter	13	Dave Cowens vs. Buffalo	March 30, 1974

MOST FREE THROWS MADE
—Game	30	Bob Cousy vs. Syracuse	March 21, 1953
—Half	12	Larry Bird vs. Detroit	April 30, 1985
—Quarter	9	Frank Ramsey vs. Minneapolis	April 4, 1959

MOST FREE THROWS ATTEMPTED
—Game	32	Bob Cousy vs. Syracuse	March 21, 1953
—Half	15	Bill Russell vs. St. Louis	April 11, 1961
—Quarter	10	Frank Ramsey vs. Minneapolis	April 4, 1959

MOST REBOUNDS
—Game	40	Bill Russell vs. Philadelphia	March 23, 1958
		Bill Russell vs. St. Louis	March 29, 1960
		Bill Russell vs. Los Angeles	April 18, 1962
—Half	25	Bill Russell vs. St. Louis	March 29, 1960
		Bill Russell vs. Los Angeles	April 18, 1962
—Quarter	19	Bill Russell vs. Los Angeles	April 18, 1962

MOST ASSISTS
—Game	19	Bob Cousy vs. St. Louis	April 9, 1957
		Bob Cousy at Minneapolis (St. Paul)	April 7, 1959
		Larry Bird vs. New York	April 28, 1990
—Half	11	Dennis Johnson vs. Los Angeles	June 7, 1985
		Bob Cousy vs. Cincinnati	April 10, 1963
		John Havlicek vs. Philadelphia	April 24, 1977
—Quarter	8	Bob Cousy vs. St. Louis	April 9, 1957
		John Havlicek vs. Philadelphia	April 24, 1977

MOST PERSONAL FOULS
—Game	6	Many players	
—Half	6	Gene Conley vs. Syracuse	March 22, 1959
		Frank Ramsey vs. Syracuse	April 1, 1959
—Quarter	5	Greg Kite at Houston	June 1, 1986

MOST CONSECUTIVE FREE THROWS MADE
	56	Bill Sharman	March 18, 1959- April 9, 1959

THREE-POINT FIELD GOALS MADE
—Game	5	Danny Ainge vs. Los Angeles	June 11, 1987
	5	Larry Bird at Milwaukee	May 18, 1986
—Half	5	Danny Ainge vs. Los angeles	June 11, 1987
—Quarter	5	Danny Ainge vs. Los Angeles	June 11, 1987
—Game, no misses	4	Scott Wedman vs. Los Angeles	May 27, 1985

THREE-POINT FIELD GOALS ATTEMPTED
—Game	8	Danny Ainge at Detroit	May 28, 1988

MOST STEALS
—Game	7	Dennis Johnson vs. Atlanta	April 29, 1986

MOST BLOCKS
—Game	7	Robert Parish vs. Philadelphia	May 9, 1982

HIGHEST FIELD GOAL PERCENTAGE
—Game	1.000	Scott Wedman vs. Los Angeles (11-for-11)	May 27, 1985

TEAM PLAYOFF RECORDS

MOST POINTS
—Game	157	vs. New York	April 28, 1990
—Half	83	vs. New York	April 28, 1990
—Quarter	46	vs. St. Louis	March 27, 1960
	46	vs. Detroit	March 24, 1968

MOST FIELD GOALS MADE
—Game	63	vs. New York	April 28, 1990
—Half	34	vs. New York	April 28, 1990
—Quarter	21	vs. Los Angeles	April 18, 1965

MOST FIELD GOALS ATTEMPTED
—Game	140	vs. Syracuse	March 18, 1959
—Half	77	vs. Philadelphia	March 22, 1960
—Quarter	42	vs. Philadelphia	March 22, 1960

MOST FREE THROWS MADE
—Game	57	vs. Syracuse	March 21, 1953
—Half	21	vs. Cleveland	April 25, 1985
—Quarter	15	vs. Cleveland	April 25, 1985

MOST FREE THROWS ATTEMPTED
—Game	64	vs. Syracuse	March 21, 1953
—Half	30	vs. St. Louis	April 9, 1958
—Quarter	18	vs. Los Angeles	April 18, 1962

MOST REBOUNDS
—Game	107	vs. Philadelphia	March 19, 1960
—Half	60	vs. Philadelphia	March 19, 1960
—Quarter	31	vs. Philadelphia	March 19, 1960
		vs. Syracuse	March 23, 1961

MOST ASSISTS
—Game	46	vs. New York	April 28, 1990
—Half	28	vs. New York	April 28, 1990
—Quarter	15	vs. New York	April 28, 1990

MOST PERSONAL FOULS
—Game	52	vs. Syracuse	March 21, 1953
—Half	21	vs. Cincinnati	March 28, 1963
—Quarter	11	vs. Los Angeles	April 17, 1966

MOST DISQUALIFICATIONS
—Game	5	vs. Syracuse	March 21, 1953

MOST CONSECUTIVE WINS
	7	vs. three teams	May 6, 1986- May 29, 1986

MOST CONSECUTIVE LOSSES
	5	vs. Detroit	June 1, 1988- May 2, 1989

THREE-POINT FIELD GOALS MADE
—Game	8	at Milwaukee	May 18, 1986

THREE-POINT FIELD GOALS ATTEMPTED
—Game	12	at Detroit	May 28, 1988
	12	at Milwaukee	May 18, 1986

MOST STEALS
—Game	15	vs. Houston	May 26, 1986
	15	vs. Atlanta	April 29, 1986
	15	vs. New York	May 9, 1984
	15	at LA Lakers	June 6, 1984

MOST BLOCKS
—Game	15	at Washington	May 1, 1982

FEWEST TURNOVERS
—Game	5	vs. Chicago	April 26, 1987

Heinsohn drives against New York's Willis Reed in 1964.

CELTICS' CAREER PLAYOFFS LEADERS

POINTS
1. Larry Bird — 3852
2. John Havlicek — 3776
3. Kevin McHale — 2941
4. Sam Jones — 2909
5. Bill Russell — 2673
6. Robert Parish — 2495
7. Tom Heinsohn — 2058
8. Bob Cousy — 2018
9. Dennis Johnson — 1733
10. Jo Jo White — 1720

AVERAGE POINTS (25 Game Min.)
1. Larry Bird — 24.1
2. John Havlicek — 22.0
3. Jo Jo White — 21.5
4. Tom Heinsohn — 19.8
5. Kevin McHale — 19.0
5. Dave Cowens — 18.9
7. Sam Jones — 18.9
8. Bill Sharman — 18.5
9. Bob Cousy — 18.5
10. Dennis Johnson — 16.7

GAMES PLAYED
1. John Havlicek — 172
2. Bill Russell — 165
3. Larry Bird — 160
5. Kevin McHale — 155
5. Robert Parish — 154
6. Sam Jones — 154
7. Don Nelson — 134
8. Tom Sanders — 130
9. Danny Ainge — 112
10. Bob Cousy — 109

MINUTES PLAYED
1. Bill Russell — 7497
2. John Havlicek — 6860
3. Larry Bird — 6779
4. Robert Parish — 5368
5. Kevin McHale — 5297
6. Sam Jones — 4654
7. Bob Cousy — 4140
8. Dennis Johnson — 4096
9. Dave Cowens — 3768
10. Jo Jo White — 3428

FREE THROWS ATTEMPTED
1. Bill Russell — 1106
2. John Havlicek — 1046
3. Larry Bird — 1008
4. Kevin McHale — 914
5. Bob Cousy — 799
6. Sam Jones — 753
7. Robert Parish — 704
8. Tom Heinsohn — 568
9. Dennis Johnson — 513
10. Frank Ramsey — 476

FREE THROWS MADE
1. Larry Bird — 898
2. John Havlicek — 874
3. Kevin McHale — 719
4. Bill Russell — 667
5. Bob Cousy — 640
6. Sam Jones — 611
7. Robert Parish — 511
8. Dennis Johnson — 429
9. Tom Heinsohn — 422
10. Frank Ramsey — 393

FREE THROW PERCENTAGE
(200 FTM Minimum)
1. Bill Sharman — .911 (370-406)
2. Larry Bird — .892 (898-1008)
3. Dennis Johnson — .836 (429-513)
4. John Havlicek — .836 (874-1046)
5. Larry Siegfried — .834 (256-307)
6. Jo Jo White — .828 (256-309)
7. Frank Ramsey — .826 (393-476)
8. Don Nelson — .819 (385-470)
9. Sam Jones — .811 (611-753)
10. Bob Cousy — .801 (640-799)

ASSISTS
1. Larry Bird — 1041
2. Bob Cousy — 937
3. John Havlicek — 825
4. Bill Russell — 770
5. Dennis Johnson — 711
6. Danny Ainge — 489
7. Jo Jo White — 452
8. K.C. Jones — 396
9. Sam Jones — 358
10. Dave Cowens — 333

FIELD GOALS ATTEMPTED
1. John Havlicek — 3329
2. Larry Bird — 3048
3. Sam Jones — 2571
4. Bill Russell — 2335
5. Tom Heinsohn — 2035
6. Bob Cousy — 2016
7. Kevin McHale — 1964
8. Robert Parish — 1855
9. Jo Jo White — 1629
10. Dave Cowens — 1627

FIELD GOALS MADE
1. John Havlicek — 1451
2. Larry Bird — 1437
3. Sam Jones — 1149
4. Kevin McHale — 1107
5. Bill Russell — 1003
6. Robert Parish — 992
7. Tom Heinsohn — 818
8. Dave Cowens — 733
9. Jo Jo White — 732
10. Bob Cousy — 689

FIELD GOAL PERCENTAGE

(200 FGM Minimum)
1. Kevin McHale — .564 (1107-1964)
2. Cedric Maxwell — .546 (356-652)
3. Robert Parish — .503 (934-1858)
4. Don Nelson — .500 (554-1109)
5. Bailey Howell — .498 (306-615)
6. Larry Bird — .471 (1437-3048)
7. Danny Ainge — .465 (479-1030)
8. Gerald Henderson — .454 (244-538)
9. Dave Cowens — .451 (733-1627)
10. Jo Jo White — .449 (732-1629)

REBOUNDS
1. Bill Russell — 4104
2. Larry Bird — 1665
3. Robert Parish — 1514
4. Dave Cowens — 1285
5. John Havlicek — 1186
6. Kevin McHale — 1157
7. Tom Heinsohn — 954
8. Tom Sanders — 763
9. Paul Silas — 763
10. Dennis Johnson — 739

PERSONAL FOULS
1. Bill Russell — 546
2. Robert Parish — 535
3. Kevin McHale — 531
4. John Havlicek — 517
5. Tom Sanders — 508
6. Larry Bird — 459
7. Tom Heinsohn — 417
8. Dave Cowens — 398
9. Sam Jones — 395
10. Frank Ramsey — 362

DISQUALIFICATIONS
1. Tom Sanders — 26
2. Dave Cowens — 15
3. Robert Parish — 15
4. Charlie Scott — 14
5. Tom Heinsohn — 14
6. Frank Ramsey — 13
7. Bailey Howell — 11
8. John Havlicek — 9
9. Bob Donham — 9
10. Bill Russell — 8
11. Jim Loscutoff — 8
12. Bob Brannum — 8
13. Kevin McHale — 8

INDIVIDUAL PLAYOFF PERFORMANCES

Scoring

54	John Havlicek, at Atlanta	April 1, 1973
51	Sam Jones, at New York	March 30, 1967
50	Bob Cousy, vs. Syracuse (4 OT)	March 21, 1953
47	Sam Jones, vs. Cincinnati	April 10, 1963

Field Goals Made

24	John Havlicek, at Atlanta	April 1, 1973
19	Sam Jones, at New York	March 30, 1967

Free Throws Made

30	Bob Cousy, vs. Syracuse (4 OT)	March 21, 1953
20	Bob Cousy, vs. Syracuse	March 17, 1954

Assists

19	Bob Cousy, vs. St. Louis	April 9, 1957
19	Bob Cousy, at Minneapolis	April 7, 1959
18	Bob Cousy, vs. Syracuse	March 18, 1959

Rebounds

40	Bill Russell, vs. Philadelphia	March 23, 1958
40	Bill Russell, vs. St. Louis	March 29, 1960
40	Bill Russell, vs. Los Angeles	April 18, 1962

OPPONENTS INDIVIDUAL PLAYOFF PERFORMANCES

Scoring

63	Michael Jordan, Chicago at Boston (2OT)	April 20, 1986
61	Elgin Baylor, Los Angeles at Boston	April 14, 1962
53	Jerry West, at Los Angeles	April 23, 1969
50	Bob Pettit, at St. Louis	April 12, 1958
50	Wilt Chamberlain, Philadelphia at Boston	March 22, 1960
49	Michael Jordan, Chicago at Boston	April 17, 1986

Field Goals Made

22	Wilt Chamberlain, Philadelphia at Boston	March 22, 1960
22	Elgin Baylor, Los Angeles at Boston	April 14, 1962
22	Michael Jordan, Chicago at Boston	April 20, 1986

Free Throws Made

21	Oscar Robertson, Cincinnati at Boston	April 10, 1963
19	Bob Pettit, St. Louis at Boston	April 9, 1958

Assists

22	Glenn Rivers, at Atlanta	May 16, 1988
21	Earvin Johnson, at Los Angeles	June 3, 1984
20	Earvin Johnson, at Los Angeles	June 4, 1987
19	Earvin Johnson, at Los Angeles	June 14, 1987

Rebounds

41	Wilt Chamberlain, at Philadelphia	April 5, 1967
39	Wilt Chamberlain, at Philadelphia	April 6, 1965
38	Wilt Chamberlain, at San Francisco	April 24, 1964

Russell defends against the Warriors' Nate Thurmond in the 1964 Finals.

Russell goes against the Lakers' Gene Wiley in the 1965 Finals.

THIS DATE IN CELTICS PLAYOFF HISTORY

Text by David Zuccaro

03/21/53 — The Boston Celtics won a playoff series for the first time with a 111-105 four overtime win over the Syracuse Nationals. Bob Cousy made 30 of 32 free throws in a 50 point performance, including a 30-foot shot at the buzzer of the third overtime which tied the game at 99. Syracuse led by 5 points, 104-99, in the fourth overtime before Boston's comeback.

03/28/48 — The Boston Celtics played their first playoff game, a 79-72 loss in Boston to the Chicago Stags.

03/31/48 — The Boston Celtics won a playoff game (second of the series) for the first time, an 81-77 victory over the Chicago Stags in Boston.

04/01/73 — John Havlicek scored a team record 54 points as the Boston Celtics defeated the Atlanta Hawks 134-109 in their playoff opener.

04/02/58 — In the third game of an eventual six games series, Bill Russell was forced out due to a severely swollen left ankle. St. Louis won the game 111-108, and the series as Russell did not return until the final game.

04/05/62 — The Boston Celtics defeated the Philadelphia Warriors 109-107 in the seventh game of their Eastern Division Final at Boston Garden. Sam Jones' 18-footer with two seconds remaining provided the victory.

04/06/57 — Coach Red Auerbach punched St. Louis Hawks owner Ben Kerner in the mouth prior to the Boston Celtics third game loss in St. Louis, 100-98. Auerbach was levied a $300 fine for the pre-game courtside incident, incensed with Kerner for what he felt were unnecessary and unfair tactics aimed at putting Boston at a disadvantage.

04/09/59 — The Boston Celtics won their 2nd NBA title, 118-113 in a four game sweep at the Minneapolis Lakers. Bill Sharman scored 29 points.

04/09/60 — One year after winning title number 2, the Boston Celtics added a third trophy with a commanding 122-103 win over the St. Louis Hawks in seven games. Frank Ramsey had a game high 24 points and Bill Russell grabbed 35 rebounds in the Boston Garden.

04/11/61 — The Boston Celtics won their 4th NBA title by downing the St. Louis Hawks 121-112 at Boston Garden in five games. Bill Russell scored 30 points and grabbed 38 rebounds.

04/11/67 — In an Eastern Division five game loss to the Philadelphia 76ers, the Boston Celtics failed to win an NBA title for the only time in the entire decade of the '60's. The Sixers, who won 140-116, outscored Boston 75-46 in the second half.

04/12/58 — The Boston Celtics were dethroned by the St. Louis Hawks in six games, 110-109. Bill Russell discarded his crutches (left ankle injury suffered on 4/2/58), but was unable to perform effectively and needed to be assisted off the floor. Bob Pettit had 50 points.

04/13/57 — The Boston Celtics won their 1st NBA title in seven games by edging the St. Louis Hawks 125-123 in 2 OT's at Boston Garden. Tom Heinsohn had 28 rebounds and 37 points to offset Bob Pettit's 39 points. Bill Sharman, who missed shots at the end of regulation and the first overtime to win the game, and Bob Cousy combined to shoot just 5-40 from the field; Bill Russell had 32 rebounds. The winning basket was made by Frank Ramsey with 1:12 left, as the game featured 38 lead changes, 28 ties, and a unique final play by St. Louis' player-coach Alex Hannum. With Boston leading by 2 points in the concluding seconds, Hannum, in his lone game of the series, planned to bounce the pass off the backboard with the hope that Pettit could tip it in. The former part of the plan worked, but the latter did not as the shot rolled off the rim.

04/15/65 — As announced by Johnny Most: "Havlicek stole the ball." John Havlicek stole Hal Greer's inbounds pass intended for Chet Walker, which enabled the Boston Celtics to defeat the Philadelphia 76ers 110-109 in the seventh game of the Eastern Division Finals at Boston Garden. Sam Jones, the recipient of Havlicek's steal, led all with 37 points. Prior to the steal, Bill Russell's attempted inbounds pass hit a guy wire, which gave the Sixers the ball down by one point with five seconds to play.

04/18/62 — The Boston Celtics won their 5th NBA title 110-107 in overtime against the Los Angeles Lakers. Boston, who had rallied from a 3-2 deficit, were led by Bill Russell's 40 rebounds and 30 points. Frank Selvy's famous missed shot occurred in this game. At the end of regulation, the Lakers guard missed at the buzzer and enabled the Celtics to eventually prevail in OT. The score was tied at 100 when Selvy missed an open 12-foot baseline jumper as the ball hit the rim, skipped across the open hole, and fell off to the delight of the Boston Garden faithful.

04/19/68 — The Boston Celtics dethroned the reigning NBA Champion Philadelphia 76ers 100-96 in the Spectrum. Seven Celtics scored in double figures as Boston won the last three games of the seven game series, to become the first team ever to accomplish that feat.

04/20/73 — The Boston Celtics lost in Boston Garden 98-91 to the New York Knicks in the third game of the Eastern Conference Finals as John Havlicek hyperextended his right shoulder fighting through a Dave DeBusschere pick. The star did not return until the fifth game at much less than 100%.

04/20/86 — Michael Jordan scored 63 points but his Chicago Bulls dropped the second game of their first round playoff battle at the Boston Celtics 135-131 in double overtime.

04/22/73 — On Easter Sunday, playing without the injured John Havlicek (right shoulder), the Boston Celtics lost at the New York Knicks 117-110 in two overtimes in the fourth game of the Eastern Conference Finals. Boston led 76-60 with 10 minutes left in regulation, but were outscored in the fourth quarter 33-17.

04/23/85 — With Larry Bird out of the lineup due to an injured elbow, Scott Wedman stepped in and scored 30 points in the third game of their best-of-five series at the Cleveland Cavaliers. Boston lost, however, 105-98.

04/24/63 — The Boston Celtics won their 6th NBA title with a 112-109 sixth game win at the Los Angeles Lakers. Bob Cousy, who scored 18 points in his final game as a Celtic, dribbled out the waning seconds and heaved the ball to the rafters as the buzzer sounded.

04/24/83 — During an on-court fight which cleared both benches, Tree Rollins of the Atlanta Hawks bit Danny Ainge on the palm side of the right index finger. This third and clinching game was played in front of a nationally televised audience as the Boston Celtics won 98-79.

04/25/65 — In Boston Garden, the Boston Celtics defeated the Los Angeles Lakers 129-96 in the fifth game of the NBA Finals, for their 8th NBA title.

04/26/64 — Despite 30 points and 27 rebounds from Wilt Chamberlain, the Boston Celtics thrilled their Boston Garden fans with a 105-99 win over the San Francisco Warriors in the fifth game of the NBA Finals. The win provided Boston with their 7th NBA title. Bill Russell had 26 rebounds and Tom Heinsohn added 19 points in Frank Ramsey's and Jim Loscutoff's career finale.

04/26/91 — Despite missing seven of the last eight regular season games, and being held to limited practice time in that span due to back spasms, Larry Bird scored 21 points with 12 rebounds and 12 assists in leading the Boston Celtics to a 127-120 win over the Indiana Pacers at Boston Garden in the first game of their best-of-five series.

04/28/66 — Red Auerbach retired as coach of the Boston Celtics after guiding them to their 8th consecutive title and 9th total, a 95-93 triumph over the Los Angeles Lakers in the seventh game of the 1966 NBA Finals. Auerbach coached Boston to nine NBA World Championships, the most any coach has won (second on the list is John Kundla with five).

04/28/90 — The Boston Celtics set a playoff scoring record by routing the New York Knicks 157-128 to take a 2-0 lead in their first round series. Boston set many team records including a league best .670 (63-94) field goal percentage.

04/28/91 — Chuck Person set an NBA record with 7 3-point field goals made in the Indiana Pacers 130-118 win in Boston Garden. The win tied the best-of-five series at one game apiece, as Person ended the afternoon with 39 points.

04/29/73 — The Boston Celtics lost the seventh game of the Eastern Conference Finals 94-78 to the New York Knicks at Boston Garden. Boston had trailed 3-1 in the series.

04/29/69 — Sam Jones connected on a last second shot which gave the Boston Celtics an 89-88 win at Boston Garden over the Los Angeles Lakers. Emmette Bryant stole the ball with seven seconds left. After a timeout, John Havlicek passed the ball to Jones, who launched an off-balance 18-footer; the ball hit the rim twice before falling and the series was tied at 2 games each.

05/02/68 — The Boston Celtics won their 10th NBA Championship with a 124-109 sixth game win at the Los Angeles Lakers. Bill Russell won the first of his two championships as a head coach.

05/03/81 — The Boston Celtics wiped out a double digit deficit in the second half for the third straight game and defeated the Philadelphia 76ers 91-90 in the seventh game of a memorable Eastern Conference Finals series. The Sixers led 89-82 with 5:23 remaining, but scored only one point in committing five turnovers and missing six shots in that stretch drive.

05/05/69 — Bill Russell and Sam Jones ended their Boston Celtics careers with a 108-106 seventh game victory over the Los Angeles Lakers to give Boston its 11th NBA World Championship in 13 years. While Russell accounted for 21 rebounds and 6 points in bowing out as a player-coach and Jones added 24 points before fouling out, it was a Don Nelson basket that finally secured the win. With little more than a minute left, after the Lakers pared the Celtics lead from 17 to 1, and with the 24-second clock winding down, Nelson's desperation 15-footer hit the back of the rim, bounced straight up about three feet, then dramatically dropped straight through the basket to give Boston a three point lead. The victory spoiled Lakers owner Jack Kent Cooke's premature celebration plans which included a marching band, and balloons prominently exhibited from the rafters.

05/05/82 — In a double overtime contest, the Boston Celtics eliminated the Washington Bullets 131-126 in Boston Garden. The Celtics won the series 4-1 in games.

05/05/91 — In dramatic fashion, Larry Bird, after a post-fourth game challenge to his hometown fans, delighted the faithful with a mid-third quarter return after a serious fall with 4:23 remaining (Boston led 48-46) in the second quarter. Bird's face made contact with the floor resulting in a bruise under the right eye, and a return unknown. Then in Superman-like custom, Bird charged out of the lockerroom resulting in mass delirium. After he re-entered the game with 6:46 left in the third quarter and Boston leading 73-71, the Celtics then went on a 39-25 run before Indiana nearly made a miraculous comeback by cutting Boston's lead to 122-121 with 3.4 seconds left. Boston barely held on to win 124-121, clinching the best of five series 3 games to 2 over the Indiana Pacers. Little-used Derek Smith made his first major impact as a Celtic as he scored a career playoff high 12 points in 22 minutes, while playing tenaciously on the defensive end.

05/06/86 — The Boston Celtics eliminated the Atlanta Hawks four game to one, 132-99 in Boston Garden. The Celtics dominated the third quarter 36-6, holding the Hawks to an all-time low quarter point production in a playoff game. In the implausible frame, Boston outscored Atlanta 34-3 at one stretch including a 24-0 run in the last 5:17 of the quarter. Boston, which led 66-55 at the half, entered the fourth quarter with a commanding 102-61 advantage.

05/06/90 — The New York Knicks concluded an improbable comeback by winning the last three games of a best-of-five series, 121-114 in Boston Garden.

05/09/81 — The Boston Celtics beat the Houston Rockets 94-71 in the third game of the NBA Finals. The Rockets 71 points matched the NBA Finals low set by the Syracuse Nationals in 1955. Houston's 30 first half points were a record low as well.

05/09/82 — The Boston Celtics defeated the Philadelphia 76ers 121-81 in Boston Garden. The series opener remains Boston's largest margin of victory in any playoff game.

05/10/74 — Kareem Abdul-Jabbar's spectacular 15-foot sky-hook from the right corner with three seconds remaining in the second overtime gave the Milwaukee Bucks a 102-101 victory over the Boston Celtics in the sixth game of their title series. Abdul-Jabbar's basket gave him 34 points in the contest, spoiling John Havlicek's magnificent corner shot over the Bucks star center with eight seconds left that gave Boston a one point lead.

05/12/74 — The Boston Celtics won their 12th championship with a 102-87 victory at the Milwaukee Bucks in the seventh game of a tremendous series. A sag defense frustrated Kareem Abdul-Jabbar as he is shut out for a pivotal 17:58 stretch from late in the first period to early in the third period in which Boston established a 17 point lead. Tom Heinsohn won the first of his two titles as a head coach.

05/14/81 — Larry Bird scored 27 points and Cedric Maxwell added 19 to lead the Boston Celtics to a 102-91 conquest over the Houston Rockets. Boston won their 14th title in six games.

05/17/87 — The Boston Celtics overcame a game Milwaukee Bucks team 119-113 in the seventh game of their Eastern Conference Semifinals series at Boston Garden. Milwaukee led by one point entering the final quarter, but Larry Bird scored 13 of his 31 points in the decisive frame. The Bucks, leading 108-100, were 0-for-10 from the floor in the final 5:25 of the game, scoring just 3 points. Danny Ainge was rendered unavailable for the final 16:43 because of a right knee injury, but replacement Jerry Sichting singes the Bucks with two key hoops during Boston's rally.

05/17/91 — For the first time since 1982, the closing game of a series involving the Boston Celtics went to an overtime period, as the Celtics fell to the World Champion Detroit Pistons 117-113 at Auburn Hills. Despite playing without an injured Robert Parish (sprained left ankle), the Celtics miraculously fought back from an 80-65 deficit with 2:47 left in the third; a lineup of McHale-Bird-Pinckney-Brown-Lewis played without a substitute for all but the final 12 seconds of OT. With 58 seconds left in regulation, a Kevin McHale tip-in was denied by referee Jack Madden due to offensive interference, although replays showed otherwise (the score was tied at 103 at the time). McHale ended the night with 34 points, Joe Dumars with 32 (25 in the first half). It was the first time since 1952 that the Celtics were eliminated from the post-season picture in an overtime game.

05/19/82 — The Boston Celtics defeated the Philadelphia 76ers 114-85 in the fifth game of the Eastern Conference Championship behind a strong defensive effort which forced the Sixers to 33% shooting from the field.

05/22/88 — In the seventh game of the Eastern Conference Semifinals won 118-116 by the Boston Celtics, the Celtics and Atlanta Hawks shot a combined .588, the second highest mark in playoff history. Larry Bird and Dominique Wilkins performed marvelously, as Bird scored 34 points (15-24, 1-3, 3-3) including 20 in the 4th quarter (9-10 field goals) and Wilkins scored 47 points (19-33, 1-2, 8-9) including 16 in the final frame. In the famous fourth quarter, the teams shoot 72% (Boston 12-15 fgs, Atlanta 14-21) from the floor in Boston Garden.

05/23/76 — Dave Cowens dominated the opener of the NBA Finals with 25 points and 21 rebounds as the Boston Celtics defeated the Phoenix Suns 98-87.

05/23/82 — The Philadelphia 76ers pulled off a rare seventh game victory in Boston Garden, beating the Boston Celtics 120-106 in the Eastern Conference Finals.

05/23/87 — Larry Bird and Bill Laimbeer were ejected for fighting in the third game of the Eastern Conference Finals at Detroit. Bird was fined $2,000 and Laimbeer $5,000. The Boston Celtics lost to the Detroit Pistons 122-104.

05/26/87 — In one of the most famous plays in basketball history, Larry Bird stole Isiah Thomas' inbounds pass with 5 seconds remaining and fed the ball over his shoulder to a cutting Dennis Johnson for the winning basket in the Boston Celtics 108-107 win over the Detroit Pistons in the fifth game of the Eastern Conference Finals. The game also featured Robert Parish's skirmish with Bill Laimbeer. For throwing punches, Parish was fined $7,500 and suspended for the next game. The fine was the second largest in league history, behind Kermit Washington's $10,000 setback (also a 60-day suspension for his actions against Rudy Tomjanovich in 1977).

05/26/88 — Exactly one year after the buzzer-beating Larry Bird-Dennis Johnson hook-up, Kevin McHale connected on a three-point field goal with 5 seconds remaining in the first overtime of the Boston Celtics eventual 119-115 double overtime victory over the Detroit Pistons in the second game of the Eastern Conference Finals.

05/27/85 — Scott Wedman shot 11-for-11 from the field, an NBA Finals record, as the Boston Celtics routed the Los Angeles Lakers 148-114 on Memorial Day. Boston's 148 points, 62 field goals made and .608 team shooting also set Finals records.

05/30/87 — Five offensive rebounds led to a Danny Ainge three point field goal with three minutes to go as the Boston Celtics rallied to beat the Detroit Pistons 117-114 in the seventh game of the Eastern Conference Finals. Ainge also made an 18-footer with 25 seconds left to make it 108-105. With 8 seconds left in the third quarter and Detroit leading 80-79, Adrian Dantley and Vinnie Johnson collided sending Dantley to the hospital with a concussion.

05/31/84 — With the Boston Celtics an apparent loser, Gerald Henderson stole James Worthy's inbounds pass to Byron Scott with 13 seconds left in the fourth quarter to tie the game at 113. The Celtics eventually won the second game 124-121 in overtime to tie the series at 1 game apiece. Uncharacteristically, Magic Johnson dribbled out the final seconds of the fourth quarter before finally passing to Bob McAdoo, whose shot was taken after the buzzer sounded. Scott Wedman's jumper with 14 seconds left gave Boston a 122-121 lead, and a Robert Parish steal from McAdoo after that protected Boston's victory.

06/04/76 — Jo Jo White scored 33 points in 60 minutes as the Boston Celtics outlasted the Phoenix Suns 128-126 in triple-overtime. The fifth game win gave Boston a 3-2 lead and featured many highlights including John Havlicek's running banker which gave Boston a 111-110 lead with 1 second remaining in the second overtime. That play was immediately followed by Paul Westphal's timeout with his knowledge that the Suns had none remaining; because of this, Boston was given a technical foul shot, which White converted, but allowed the Suns to inbound the ball from center court rather than under their own defensive basket. Gar Heard's improbable 22-foot launch at the buzzer tied the score at 112 and sent the game to a third overtime session, where little used Glenn McDonald, replacing Paul Silas who fouled out, attained instant hero status by scoring six crucial points in the decisive drive.

06/05/85 — Dennis Johnson's buzzer-beating jumpshot gave the Boston Celtics a 107-105 win at the Los Angeles Lakers to tie the NBA Finals at 2 games apiece.

Russell blocks a shot by the Lakers' Archie Marshall in the 1968 Finals.

06/05/86 — Ralph Sampson was ejected for fighting, mainly with Jerry Sichting, but the Houston Rockets won the fifth game of the NBA Finals 111-96 at Houston.

06/06/76 — Charlie Scott's 25 points paced the Boston Celtics to an 87-80 sixth game win at the Phoenix Suns. Boston's win marked the franchise's 13th title in history.

06/06/84 — The Boston Celtics beat the Los Angeles Lakers in overtime 129-125 at the Forum to tie the NBA Finals at two games apiece. M.L. Carr's key steal - and eventual dunk - of James Worthy's inbounds pass with six seconds left in the extra frame secured the win. Other highlights of this fourth game: Larry Bird's 21 rebounds and Kevin McHale's take-down of Kurt Rambis.

06/08/84 — With the temperature inside a crazed Boston Garden reaching 97 degrees, the Boston Celtics defeated the Los Angeles Lakers 121-103 in the fifth game of the NBA Finals. Larry Bird had 34 points.

06/08/86 — Larry Bird's 29 points, 12 assists, and 11 rebounds helped the Boston Celtics beat the Houston Rockets 114-97 to wrap up their 16th NBA title. Bird also won the playoff MVP for the second time in three years.

06/11/87 — Five Boston Celtics players reached the 20 point figure, led by Dennis Johnson's 25, to tie an NBA Finals record. Boston beat the Los Angeles Lakers 123-108 at Boston Garden in the fifth game.

06/12/84 — Cedric Maxwell had 24 points, 8 rebounds, and 8 assists and the Boston Celtics outrebounded the Los Angeles Lakers 52-33 in a 111-102 seventh game victory at Boston Garden. The Celtics, winners of their 15th NBA title, were the guests of President Ronald Reagan at the White House a day later.

CELTICS WORLD CHAMPIONSHIP TEAMS

1956-57
(44-28* regular season, 7-3 playoffs)
Coach: Red Auerbach
Bob Cousy (64 games), Tom Heinsohn (72), Dick Hemric (67), Jim Loscutoff (70), Jack Nichols (61), Togo Palazzi (20), Andy Phillip (67), Frank Ramsey (35), Arnie Risen (43), Bill Russell (48), Bill Sharman (67) and Lou Tsioropoulos (52). Trainer: Harvey Cohn.

1958-59
(52-20* regular season, 8-3 playoffs)
Coach: Red Auerbach
Gene Conley (50 games), Bob Cousy (65), Tom Heinsohn (66), K.C. Jones (49), Sam Jones (71), Jim Loscutoff (66), Frank Ramsey (72), Bill Russell (70), Bill Sharman (72), Ben Swain (58) and Lou Tsioropoulos (35). Trainer: Buddy LeRoux.

1959-60
(59-16* regular season, 8-5 playoffs)
Coach: Red Auerbach
Gene Conley (71 games), Bob Cousy (75), Gene Guarilia (48), Tom Heinsohn (75), K.C. Jones (74), Sam Jones (74), Maurice King (1), Jim Loscutoff (28), Frank Ramsey (73), John Richter (66), Bill Russell (74) and Bill Sharman (71). Trainer: Buddy LeRoux.

1960-61
(57-22* regular season, 8-5 playoffs)
Coach: Red Auerbach
Gene Conley (75 games), Bob Cousy (76), Gene Guarilia (25), Tom Heinsohn (74), K.C. Jones (78), Sam Jones (78), Jim Loscutoff (76), Frank Ramsey (79), Bill Russell (78), Tom Sanders (68) and Bill Sharman (61). Trainer: Buddy LeRoux.

1961-62
(62-20* regular season, 8-6 playoffs)
Coach: Red Auerbach
Carl Braun (48 games), Bob Cousy (75), Gene Guarilia (45), Tom Heinsohn (79), K.C. Jones (80), Sam Jones (78), Jim Loscutoff (76), Gary Phillips (67), Frank Ramsey (79), Bill Russell (76) and Tom Sanders (80). Trainer: Buddy LeRoux.

1962-63
(58-22* regular season, 8-5 playoffs)
Coach: Red Auerbach
Bob Cousy (76 games), Gene Guarilia (11), John Havlicek (80), Tom Heinsohn (76), K.C. Jones (79), Sam Jones (76), Jim Loscutoff (63), Clyde Lovellette (61), Frank Ramsey (77), Bill Russell (78), Tom Sanders (80) and Dan Swartz (39). Trainer: Buddy LeRoux.

1963-64
(59-21* regular season, 8-2 playoffs)
Coach: Red Auerbach
John Havlicek (80 games), Tom Heinsohn (76), K.C. Jones (80), Sam Jones (76), Jim Loscutoff (53), Clyde Lovellette (45), Johnny McCarthy (28), Willie Naulls (78), Frank Ramsey (75), Bill Russell (78), Tom Sanders (80) and Larry Siegfried (31). Trainer: Buddy LeRoux.

1964-65
(62-18* regular season, 8-4 playoffs)
Coach: Red Auerbach
Ron Bonham (37 games), Mel Counts (54), John Havlicek (75), Tom Heinsohn (67), K.C. Jones (78), Sam Jones (80), Willie Naulls (71), Bob Nordmann (3), Bill Russell (78), Tom Sanders (80), Larry Siegfried (72), John Thompson (64) and Gerry Ward (3). Trainer: Buddy LeRoux.

1965-66
(54-26, 2nd in East one game behind Philadelphia in regular season, 11-6 playoffs) Coach: Red Auerbach
Ron Bonham (39 games), Mel Counts (67), Sihugo Green (10), John Havlicek (71), K.C. Jones (80), Sam Jones (67), Willie Naulls (71), Don Nelson (75), Bill Russell (78), Tom Sanders (72), Woody Sauldsberry (39), Larry Siegfried (71), John Thompson (10) and Ron Watts (1). Trainer: Buddy LeRoux.

1967-68
(54-28, 2nd in East eight games behind Philadephia regular season; 12-7 in playoffs) Player-Coach: Bill Russell
Wayne Embry (78 games), Mal Graham (78), John Havlicek (82), Bailey Howell (82), Johnny Jones (51), Sam Jones (73), Don Nelson (82), Bill Russell (78), Tom Sanders (78), Larry Siegfried (62), Tom Thacker (65) and Rick Weitzman (25). Trainer: Joe DeLauri.

1968-69
(48-34, 4th in East nine games behind first-place Baltimore regular season; 12-6 in playoffs) Player-Coach: Bill Russell
Jim Barnes (49 games), Emmette Bryant (80), Don Chaney (20), Mal Graham (22), John Havlicek (82), Bailey Howell (78), Rich Johnson (31), Sam Jones (70), Don Nelson (82), Bud Olsen (7), Bill Russell (77), Tom Sanders (82) and Larry Siegfried (79). Trainer: Joe DeLauri.

1973-74
(56-26 regular season, 12-6 playoffs)
Coach: Tom Heinsohn

Assistant Coach: John Killilea
Don Chaney (81 games), Dave Cowens (80), Steve Downing (24), Henry Finkel (60), Phil Hankinson (28), John Havlicek (76), Steve Kuberski (78), Don Nelson (82), Paul Silas (82), Paul Westphal (82), Jo Jo White (82) and Art Williams (67). Trainer: Frank Challant. Assistant Trainer: Mark Volk.

1975-76
 (54-28 regular season, 12-6 playoffs)
Coach: Tom Heinsohn
Assistant Coach: John Killilea
Jerome Anderson (22 games), Jim Ard (81), Tom Boswell (35), Dave Cowens (78), John Havlicek (76), Steve Kuberski (60), Glenn McDonald (75), Don Nelson (75), Charlie Scott (82), Ed Searcy (4), Paul Silas (81), Kevin Stacom (77) and Jo Jo White (82). Trainer: Frank Challant. Assistant Trainer: Mark Volk.

1980-81
(62-20** regular season, 12-5 playoffs)
Coach: Bill Fitch
Assistant Coaches: K.C. Jones and Jim Rodgers
Nate Archibald (80 games), Larry Bird (82), M.L. Carr (41), Terry Duerod (32), Eric Fernsten (45), Chris Ford (82), Gerald Henderson (82), Wayne Kreklow (25), Cedric Maxwell (81), Kevin McHale (82), Robert Parish (82) and Rick Robey (82). Trainer: Ray Melchiorre.

1983-84
(62-20* regular season, 15-8 playoffs)
Coach: K.C. Jones
Assistant Coaches: Jim Rodgers and Chris Ford
Danny Ainge (71 games), Larry Bird (79), Quinn Buckner (79), M.L. Carr (60), Carlos Clark (31), Gerald Henderson (78), Dennis Johnson (80), Greg Kite (35), Cedric Maxwell (80), Kevin McHale (82), Robert Parish (80) and Scott Wedman (68). Trainer: Ray Melchiorre.

1985-86
(67-15* regular season, 15-3 playoffs)
Coach: K.C. Jones
Assistant Coaches: Jim Rodgers and Chris Ford
Danny Ainge (80 games), Larry Bird (82), Rick Carlisle (77), Dennis Johnson (78), Greg Kite (64), Kevin McHale (68), Robert Parish (81), Jerry Sichting (82), David Thirdkill (49), Sam Vincent (57), Bill Walton (80), Scott Wedman (79) and Sly Williams (6), Trainer Ray Melchiorre.
 *Best record in the NBA
**tied for best record in NBA

Auerbach gets a ride off the Garden floor in 1963.

1991-92 BOSTON CELTICS SCHEDULE

				Time	

NOVEMBER - 1991

Fri.	1	— H	CHARLOTTE	7:30	
Sat.	2	— A	WASHINGTON	7:30	
Tue.	5	— A	MIAMI	8:00	
Wed.	6	— H	CHICAGO	7:30	
Fri.	8	— H	ATLANTA	7:30	
Sun.	10	— A	PORTLAND	5:00	
Tue.	12	— A	SACRAMENTO	7:30	
Wed.	13	— A	PHOENIX	7:30	
Fri.	15	— H	PHILADELPHIA	7:30	
Sat.	16	— A	CHARLOTTE	7:30	
Wed.	20	— H	INDIANA	7:30	
Sat.	23	— A	NEW JERSEY	7:30	
Mon.	25	— *	WASHINGTON	7:30	
Wed.	27	— H	ORLANDO	7:30	
Fri.	29	— H	LA LAKERS	8:00	
Sat.	30	— A	ATLANTA	7:30	

DECEMBER - 1991

Wed.	4	— H	MIAMI	7:30	
Fri.	6	— H	NEW YORK	7:30	
Mon.	9	— H	DENVER	7:30	
Fri.	13	— H	SEATTLE	7:30	
Sat.	14	— A	NEW YORK	7:30	
Tue.	17	— A	ORLANDO	7:30	
Wed.	18	— H	MILWAUKEE	7:30	
Fri.	20	— H	UTAH	7:30	
Sat.	21	— A	MIAMI	7:30	
Wed.	25	— A	CHICAGO	8:00	
Fri.	27	— A	SEATTLE	7:00	
Sat.	28	— A	DENVER	7:00	
Mon.	30	— A	LA CLIPPERS	7:30	

JANUARY - 1992

Fri.	3	— H	CLEVELAND	7:30	
Sat.	4	— A	MINNESOTA	7:00	
Mon.	6	— H	SACRAMENTO	7:30	
Wed.	8	— H	NEW YORK	7:30	
Fri.	10	— H	MINNESOTA	7:30	
Sat.	11	— A	NEW YORK	7:30	
Wed.	15	— H	NEW JERSEY	7:30	
Fri.	17	— H	PHILADELPHIA	7:30	
Sun.	19	— H	SAN ANTONIO	5:00	
Mon.	20	— A	CLEVELAND	3:30	
Wed.	22	— H	ORLANDO	7:30	
Fri.	24	— H	PHOENIX	7:30	
Sun.	26	— H	DETROIT	12:30	
Tue.	28	— A	WASHINGTON	7:30	
Fri.	31	— A	MILWAUKEE	7:00	

FEBRUARY - 1992

Sat.	1	— A	PHILADELPHIA	7:30	
Wed.	5	— H	HOUSTON	8:00	x
Tue.	11	— A	SAN ANTONIO	7:00	x
Wed.	12	— A	DALLAS	7:30	
Fri.	14	— A	HOUSTON	7:30	
Sun.	16	— A	LA LAKERS	12:30	
Mon.	17	— A	UTAH	7:30	
Wed.	19	— A	GOLDEN STATE	5:00	x
Fri.	21	— *	CHARLOTTE	7:30	x
Sun.	23	— A	INDIANA	1:00	
Tue.	25	— A	NEW JERSEY	7:30	
Wed.	26	— H	INDIANA	7:30	
Fri.	28	— A	ATLANTA	8:00	x

MARCH - 1992

Sun.	1	— H	DALLAS	7:30	
Wed.	4	— H	ORLANDO	7:30	
Fri.	6	— H	LA CLIPPERS	7:30	
Sun.	8	— A	ORLANDO	7:30	
Tue.	10	— A	MIAMI	7:30	
Wed.	11	— A	CHICAGO	7:00	x
Fri.	13	— *	NEW JERSEY	7:30	
Sun.	15	— H	PORTLAND	12:00	
Tue.	17	— A	MILWAUKEE	7:30	
Wed.	18	— H	CLEVELAND	7:30	
Fri.	20	— A	DETROIT	8:00	
Sun.	22	— H	GOLDEN STATE	2:30	
Wed.	25	— A	NEW JERSEY	7:30	
Fri.	27	— H	DETROIT	7:30	
Sun.	29	— H	ATLANTA	7:30	

APRIL - 1992

Wed.	1	— H	WASHINGTON	7:30	
Fri.	3	— A	INDIANA	8:00	x
Sun.	5	— H	CHICAGO	12:00	
Tue.	7	— A	CLEVELAND	7:30	
Wed.	8	— H	NEW YORK	7:30	
Fri.	10	— H	MILWAUKEE	7:30	
Sun.	12	— A	CHARLOTTE	6:00	
Tue.	14	— A	PHILADELPHIA	7:30	
Wed.	15	— A	DETROIT	8:00	x
Sun.	19	— H	MIAMI	1:00	

* — An asterisk denotes a home game in Hartford, CT.
All games on WEEI-Radio (590 AM).
All times listed are in the city of the game, are PM.
All times are subject to change.